CORPORATE REPORTING OF NONFINANCIAL PERFORMANCE INDICATORS AND OPERATING MEASURES

Julia Grant

Timothy Fogarty

Robert Bricker

Gary Previts

Weatherhead School of Management
Case Western Reserve University

A publication of Financial Executives Research Foundation, Inc.

Financial Executives Research Foundation, Inc.
10 Madison Avenue
P.O. Box 1938
Morristown, NJ 07962-1938
(973) 898-4608

Copyright © 2000 by Financial Executives Research Foundation, Inc.

All rights reserved. No part of this book may be reproduced in any form or by any means without written permission from the publisher.

International Standard Book Number 1-885065-17-5
Library of Congress Catalog Card Number 99-76921
Printed in the United States of America

First Printing

Financial Executives Research Foundation, Inc. (FERF®) is the research affiliate of Financial Executives Institute. The basic purpose of the Foundation is to sponsor research and publish informative material in the field of business management, with particular emphasis on the practice of financial management and its evolving role in the management of business.

The views set forth in this publication are those of the authors and do not necessarily represent those of the FERF Board as a whole, individual trustees, or the members of the Advisory Committee.

FERF publications can be ordered by calling 1-800-680-FERF
(U.S. and Canada only; international orders, please call 770-751-1986).
Quantity discounts are available.

Cover design by Mark Tocchet

ADVISORY COMMITTEE

Walter C. Wilson (Chairman)
Senior Vice President & Chief Financial Officer
EOG Resources, Inc.

Robert J. Dickson
Vice President & Treasurer
Carpenter Technology Corporation

Earnest J. Edwards
Senior Vice President & Controller (retired)
Aluminum Company of America

J. James Lewis
Executive Vice President (retired)
Financial Executives Research Foundation, Inc.

Janet Luallen
Director—Technical Activities
Financial Executives Institute

William M. Sinnett
Project Manager
Financial Executives Research Foundation, Inc.

Rhona L. Ferling
Publications Manager
Financial Executives Research Foundation, Inc.

CONTENTS

APPENDICES

INTRODUCTION

Globalization, economic development, information technologies and other factors have led to a world in which substantial, and often nontraditional, information is needed about companies for investment and other purposes. Company annual reports have the capacity to voluntarily communicate valuable information about a public company, mandated and legal disclosure requirements aside. The scope and format of these communications is very much within the discretion of the company. This discretion is often exercised to convey to the reader the company's view of itself, including its past, present, and future. In effect, the reader experiences the company through the annual report, and in this sense, annual reports can be quite distinctive.

For many years there has been a plethora of books, articles, and research studies related to company annual reporting. Some recent relevant literature is discussed in appendix A. This study focuses on nonfinancial performance indicators and operating measures reported by companies in their 1992 and 1997 annual reports. These indicators and measures are generally nonmandated qualitative and quantitative disclosures communicated by companies in the president/CEO's letter, in management discussion and analysis (MD&A), or in other areas of the annual report, excluding financial statements and notes. A case study approach was applied to a sample of 16 *Fortune* 500 companies in eight industries, as shown in table 1, to assess their disclosure of these indicators and measures. A detailed discussion of the methods employed in this study is contained in appendix B, and some introductory materials related to the sample companies are presented in appendix C.

Table 1
Sample Description
Firm Size and Industry

Industry	Company 1	*Fortune* 1997 Rank	Market Capitalization *(billions)*	Company 2	*Fortun* 1997 Rank
Beverage	PepsiCo	31	54.448	Coca-Cola	68
Chemical	DuPont	15	67.841	Dow	60
Computer	IBM	6	101.287	Dell	125
Electrical	GE	5	239.539	Rockwell	131
Food	ConAgra	45	14.373	Hershey	345
Pharmaceutical	Merck	46	126.527	Pharmacia & Upjohn	240
Paper	Champion	277	4.356	Westvaco	472
Retail	Wal-Mart	4	89.219	Sears	16

Market Capitalization *(billions)*	Industry Rank Range	Rank Multiple *(rank2/rank1)*	*Within* Fortune *Ranges*				
			1–100	*200*	*300*	*400*	*500*
164.759	37	2.2	2				
22.885	45	4.0	2				
32.019	119	20.8	1	1			
13.015	126	26.2	1	1			
8.853	300	7.7	1			1	
18.585	194	5.2	1		1		
3.345	195	1.7			1		1
17.688	12	4.0	2				

KEY FINDINGS

1. A case-study approach was used to examine the content of annual reports. The analysis showed that the content and format of annual reports are contingent on company culture, management, performance, regulatory requirements, and a variety of other factors.
2. The profitability of companies does not systematically affect the amount of their current-year disclosures. However, profitability does seem to affect the composition of disclosures. In loss years, management tends to focus on improving performance. Accordingly, a more pronounced future orientation to the report's information is evident when corporate profitability is low.
3. On average, more than half of all the nonfinancial performance indicators and operating measures identified in the study are located in the "other narrative" sections (compared with the president/CEO's letter, MD&A, and financial statements). This finding suggests the importance of discretionary narratives in company annual reports, an area that is supplemental to the content required and mandated.
4. The proportions of nonfinancial performance indicators and operating measures identified in the study are relatively consistent across information categories between 1992 and 1997.
5. Companies tend to provide more detail about their products and services than any other aspect of their operations. Companies also provide considerable detail about their markets and industries.
6. Overall, more than 30 percent of the nonfinancial performance indicators and operating measures identified in the study are located in the MD&A. While the "other narrative" category contains more items, it often comprises several sections. Therefore, we conclude that the MD&A as a single section contains the largest amount of information.

7. While specific, forward-looking forecasts are reported only sparingly, company annual reports do contain a relatively larger amount of qualitative, future-oriented discussion of company products, strategies, plans, expected performance, and other matters. Nevertheless, no consistent pattern to these discussions could be discerned.
8. Changes in the composition of the company have an impact on the content of the annual report. However, it is difficult to predict exactly how the report will be affected.

ANALYSIS OF KEY FINDINGS

Public company annual reports have attracted a great deal of attention and discussion during the past 20 years. (See appendix A for a discussion of some pertinent studies of financial reporting and a general review of related literature.) One ongoing discussion has addressed the adequacy of annual reports for investors and other parties. Another dialogue stems from companies' interest in improving their corporate communications. Both issues are grounded, to a large extent, in a world in which economic conditions and information/communication technologies are more dynamic than ever. Today, capital markets are increasingly global, corporate restructurings are widespread, investment funds of various types dominate securities transactions, Web and other communication technologies expedite capital markets trading, and federal tort laws have changed dramatically.

These and other factors have led in the 1990s to fundamental reconsideration of corporate communications. Such reconsiderations have included (among others) the development of a model for business reporting and the use of nonfinancial performance indicators and operating measures for assessing both the historical performance and the future prospects of companies. These trends provide a powerful impetus for a focused examination of the content of annual reports, which continue to be an important source of information. From the perspective of companies, it is particularly important to understand how other companies use annual reports to convey information that improves communications with investors and other parties.

This book seeks to improve understanding of nonfinancial performance indicators and operating measures contained in company annual reports. Examples of nonfinancial performance indicators and operating measures include discussions of company strategies; quality-related awards; environmental goals and performance; use of measures such as economic value added; future-oriented material such as new products and specific forward-looking forecasts; disclosure of non-generally accepted accounting principles (GAAP); and "cash flow performance equivalents" such as earnings before interest, taxes, depreciation, and amortization (EBITDA). In addition to studying annual report content, this book addresses presentation forms used by companies in their annual reports—for example, in terms of organization, length, and presentation style—as a disclosure element.

The project was conducted by studying and comparing the contents of a sample of 16 major, publicly held company annual reports in eight industries for fiscal years 1992 and 1997 (the most current reports available at the time this project was undertaken). A list of the companies selected and the details of our sample selection process can be found in appendix B. The results of the analysis provide evidence of the current state of disclosure, innovation, experimentation, and development in both the form and content of annual reports, specifically as reflected by nonfinancial performance indicators and operating measures.

Company Themes

The annual report is often used to communicate the company's vision of itself and its mission. From this perspective, the perception of the company that the annual report conveys may be created, in part, by the company's use of an explicit theme. Companies vary both in their use of discernible themes and in the extent to which themes are employed throughout an annual report. Although a theme does not change a company's underlying characteristics, it can communicate these characteristics to readers in evocative and memorable ways.

In our sample, the following examples illustrate types of themes used to create a strong image of the company:

1. Describing a specific quality control commitment, program, and process.
2. Communicating a movement toward globalization of the enterprise and specific plans for achieving globalization.
3. Detailing an array of in-process, new, and existing products.
4. Conveying a high level of technological sophistication.

Such themes and images are useful tools in shaping the messages conveyed by the annual report, and to be most effective, they must permeate all aspects. However, it is difficult to design an annual report with evocative images and a memorable theme, and the extent of information within a report does not depend on whether a company has established (or even has attempted to establish) a strong theme or image. Furthermore, some factors may impede the establishment of a distinctive theme in an annual report. These include the following:

1. Poor company performance.
2. Diffuse business focus.
3. Lack of distinct direction.

General Level of Detail

Most annual reports provide a considerable amount of detail about selected aspects of the company. However, the relative level of detail tends to vary by type of information, industry, and company. Companies provide a great deal of information about some aspects of themselves and far less about others. Examples of areas in which companies could provide detail include line of business, geographic segment, products, revenues and expenses, and assets and liabilities (including expansions and capital expenditures).

The largest amount of detail that companies consistently provide pertains to their products and services. Product development sections, in which future products are described and product potential is examined in detail, are a frequent offering, especially for companies with key strengths in science and technology. Successful products tend to be more fully described, but in-development products are often described in great detail, as in the case of pharmaceutical companies. There is relatively little discussion of unsuccessful products. The introduction of new products is frequently mentioned, but the phase-out of old products is much more selectively treated.

Companies also provide considerable detail about their markets and industries. Companies seek to convey their understanding of their markets and the key elements to being successful in those markets, and they describe their proactive stance with regard to opportunities. Companies with relatively dominant competitive positions tend to disclose market share information for related products. Geographic market share information, although less frequently seen, is not unusual; it is more common to see disclosures related to the proportion of income generated in geographic areas. Some of the industry information tends to be future oriented, in the form of commentary regarding ongoing trends (prices, costs). As part of their industry assessment, companies often provide information about their relationships with other companies. Primarily, this information involves discussion of joint ventures and strategic alliances with other companies.

Segment-level financial and nonfinancial detail is frequently found in annual reports. Very often the profitability and volume activity of divisions, product lines, or other distinguishable units are provided in narrative form. These disclosures tend to have a comparative element so that readers can judge the direction of sales and the location of the company's profitability. It is interesting to note that the businesses discussed in narratives are often different from the reportable segments defined by GAAP and reported in the MD&A section; both sampled years occur prior to the implementation of SFAS 131, "Disclosure about Segments of an Enterprise and Related Information," which defines operating segments and requires specific financial and descriptive disclosures for reportable operating segments. Segment information in other narratives is typically not additive or mathematically combinable, especially because a comparable set of information using conventional accounting is not used in all cases.

A lesser degree of information is usually available about other topics, although this varies substantially across companies. Descriptions of the nonproduct properties of the company depend on the nature of the firm's business. For example, uses of novel forms of information technology to better control or manage are sometimes presented. Information about the company's marketing efforts also varies. Future-oriented information, such as new products and facilities (which can be contrasted with more precise forward-looking forecasts) permeates many reports. More specific forward-looking predictions appear less frequently, and these disclosures are neither systematic nor comparable. Examples include general predictions about the likely prospects for company sales and profitability and expectations about the general business climate. Finally, considerable variation exists in how much strategic information is provided. This information tends to be general and nonquantified and often amounts to an indication of corporate priorities.

A third level of detail pertains to the topics that are rarely mentioned in the annual reports we examined. Modest amounts of information can be found about corporate structure, shareholders, or employees. Corporate structure tends to be mentioned only in relation to major divestitures or mergers. Information is provided to shareholders, but rarely is there any discussion about ownership structure (for example, insiders, institutional investors, and individual investors). Finally, most companies profess the value of their employees. However, specific information tends to be confined to raw employee numbers. It is more common to see brief articles about the roles of individual employees in a company.

Report Structures

The potential locations of information within the annual report are the president/CEO's letter, MD&A, other narrative, and financial statements. A preliminary reading of several annual reports suggested that the contents of the financial statements and notes are principally required disclosures. Accordingly, this project focused on the information included in other sections of the report. Nonetheless, the researchers continued to review the notes section for exceptional information.

Both MD&A and the president/CEO's letter are well-defined sections of the annual report. In contrast, the "other narrative" category incorporates all other narrative sections, including pictures and stand-alone tables and graphs, and excludes only the financial statements and notes. Most reports include at least one substantive narrative section that contains considerable content.

On average, more than half of all the coded nonfinancial performance indicators and operating measures are located in the other narrative sections. This finding suggests the importance of discretionary narratives in company annual reports, an area that is supplemental to the mandated content. Companies use this area of the annual report to describe themselves in nontraditional ways.

Overall, more than 30 percent of the nonfinancial performance indicators and operating measures are located in MD&A. While the other narrative category contains more items, it often comprises several sections. Therefore, we conclude that MD&A contains the greatest number of such disclosures to be found in a single report section.

Unlike the other narrative category, MD&A does not involve the summation of different textual elements. Therefore, on a per-page basis, MD&A provides an important amount of information.

The president/CEO's letter contains less than 15 percent of the information items that we identified in the annual reports. This does not suggest that the information found there is less important. Rather, the president/CEO's letter tends to describe the company broadly and strategically, and is less focused on individual disclosure items. Perhaps it is fair to say that the president/CEO's letter captures the principal aspects of the annual report and leaves the detail for the body of the report.

The information items in the president/CEO's letter, MD&A, and other narrative sections are classified into 1 of 11 categories, as shown in table 4 in appendix B. Most of the information in annual reports tends to fall within two categories: nonmandated financial information, and products and productive processes. On average, between 25 and 30 percent of all coded information items can be classified as additional financial information. This includes, but is not limited to, segment-level and product-level accounting/financial information. Quite often, companies report changes in profitability and revenues attributed to these units. Between 15 and 20 percent of all information items are related to descriptions of products and productive processes. Most of this category tends to be related to the announcements of new products, descriptions of new functionality for existing products, or products in development. Together, these two areas provide the largest amount of information, comprising about half of the information items in the annual reports studied.

Although no other of the 11 categories exceeds 10 percent, 4 contain roughly 8 to 9 percent of the coded information items in the annual reports. One example, relationships with other parties, is discussed in different ways across our sample. In this category, companies often discuss strategic alliances with others, as well as ongoing and future joint ventures. This area also includes relationships with governmental regulatory bodies, environmental issues, and community activities. Another area of similar importance is description of business and properties. In contrast to the detail communicated about products, this category focuses on company-wide information. It includes descriptions of plants and other productive facilities, descriptions of the geographical dispersion of the company, and breakdowns of firm-wide revenues. The third category of similar importance involves industry information. Companies that provide market share data illustrate this category of information. This category can also include discussion of industry demand, price levels, and other important trends faced by the company and its competitors. Finally, future-oriented and forward-looking information is of similar importance. This information includes the company's qualitative or quantitative impression of its future. It includes relatively "hard" information, such as the expected completion date for a new factory, as well as "soft" information, such as a prediction that raw material prices will change in the near term.

Several categories contain less than 5 percent of the total information items. Information about investors or shareholders is one such category. Similarly, there is relatively little information about company personnel in annual reports, although notable exceptions occur in the form of articles describing individual employee activities in a company. Somewhat more information is provided about corporate board members and key officers. Sometimes this includes background information and responsibilities (for example, board committee memberships). Annual reports also generally do not describe company marketing. Retail industry companies are notable exceptions, devoting other narrative sections to their marketing efforts. More commonly, oblique references are made to marketing efforts and product promotion. Finally, strategic plan information is not found in great detail in annual reports, although all companies provide a broad picture of their strategies.

Relatively Unique Content

Every company has notable content or presentation. Some of this information pertains to the measurement of performance. Some is related to the numbers by which firms manage their businesses, and therefore offers readers valuable insights. Some of the unique content is appropriate for a given industry and, therefore, could not be applied similarly elsewhere.

The nature of unique content is such that it is difficult to synthesize or summarize across the entire sample of companies in a meaningful way. There is even some difficulty in discussing unique content outside of the context and time period of the company's annual report. To discuss this information, the traditional financial information also found in annual reports can serve as a benchmark. The unique content in these documents can be appreciated best by comparing it with mandated financial disclosures and traditional presentation forms.

Several companies report proprietary calculations based almost exclusively on accounting information. Sometimes these measures unravel the impact of noncash expenses. At other times, they add in other effects, such as income taxes, that are often obscured in some financial statements. Examples of these include alternative measures of free cash flows and economic value added. Perhaps the most interesting aspect of these measures is the fact that the company expresses great confidence in them and apparently manages with their guidance.

Some reports use traditional accounting data in new ways, sometimes combining one piece of accounting information with a nonfinancial metric. Several companies report productivity measures, usually using a denominator such as number of employees or number of labor hours. Companies that include information about backlogged orders are also using a variant of traditional accounting. Expressions of sales and other activities on a per capita basis employ various demographic tools to enhance the reader's appreciation. In this study, such information is typically coded as production information or as nonmandated financial information, depending on the context within the report (see appendix B).

Some unique information is actually traditional information in a new format. Company results that are disaggregated across different parts of the firm fit into this category. In addition to segmenting the firm along product lines and groups of related product lines, some attention is given to separating non-U.S. and U.S. accounting results, and state or regional results. Multiple ways to organize the same activity (e.g., by product or geographical area) allow the company more flexibility in conveying its performance.

Information is also assembled and portrayed in unique presentation formats, including innovative use of tables, graphs, and narratives that—in conjunction with information content—illuminate particular aspects of the companies' operations. For example, some companies provide thumbnail organizational sketches of their various lines of business that include (among other items) summary financial information, strategy, key products, prospects, and relationship with other lines of business.

Another group of notable items involves logical extensions of accounting information. For example, several firms use physical measures to track the accomplishment of their objectives. This controls for the price variations that would be included in more conventionally denominated (e.g., money) measures. Another type of comment in this group pertains to productive capacity, such as specific facility plans and store openings. The conventional focus on performance is supplemented by future-oriented information that provides a more complete picture of company prospects.

Some of the unique disclosures involve an attempt to look beyond the traditional numbers. Since not everything can be well quantified, adequate communication sometimes suggests the need for narrative or quantitative elaboration. Examples include the impact of past mergers, the value and duration of intellectual property rights, and changes in the company's capital structure. Although related information can be found in traditional accounting disclosures (as amplified by the notes to the financial statements), supplemental treatments not only draw attention to such issues, but also increase the qualitative dimension that, in many instances, would otherwise be lost. Management can successfully point out the hidden dimensions that accounting cannot, especially when they infuse the annual report with expressions of their expectations, their midcourse corrections, and their reasoning that balances short- and long-term objectives. Some of the best work in this area draws upon research about relationships between different informational units. An example is product life cycle analysis.

The success of any company depends in part on the caliber of its relationships with others. Accordingly, companies use the annual report to describe in qualitative terms the importance and success of such relationships. This content, albeit important, ranges far from conventional accounting information. It includes evaluation of the company by external parties. When this coalesces into a certification, a ranking, or an award, it takes on the hard edge of an objective fact that can be pointed out by management. An example is an ISO (International Standards Organization) 9000 quality certification. Measures of customer satisfaction are also in this category. The "softer" version is customer testimonials, which, despite their anecdotal nature, attest to valuable goodwill.

Relationships with employees are also described. This may range from descriptions of their caliber to efforts that are being made to make them more productive. A third type of relationship pertains to the government. Typically, this takes the form of describing the successful navigation of regulatory structures. Examples include product safety approval and passing critical tests stipulated by contract. Some companies used unique content to assure readers that environmental performance was not only adequate, but in excess of the minimum. Notable in this area are companies that take a potential negative and create a positive in terms of environmental conservation.

Structure of the Reports

Although the case studies reveal considerable variation in how the annual report is structured, they also suggest broad common features. Table 3 summarizes the components of the annual reports of our sample companies.

Reports typically begin with a brief tabular array of financial highlights. This functions as a sort of executive summary for those who want only a general overview of the year's performance. The first substantive section tends to be a president/CEO's letter. Letters average four to six pages in length and address several matters, including setting a focus or perspective for the reader in interpreting the rest of the report, stressing the highlights of company performance, and discussing any major changes in the structure or direction of the company. The material that follows the president/CEO's letter constitutes the beginning of the other narrative section.

The other narrative section may consist of one or multiple subsections. Some companies provide general narratives. Some sections are organized thematically—for example, in terms of products, strategy, and marketing. Others are organized by segments, divisions, markets, or product category. One common feature in this part of the report is the relatively larger number of pictures and graphic displays.

There is no uniform order for the remaining components of the annual report. Most often, the next substantive section is the MD&A, which is sometimes given a different title (e.g., financial review). This section tends to concentrate on financial matters and to be more technical and quantitative. Positioned as it is, some of its information repeats material covered elsewhere, particularly in the other narrative section.

The standard disclaimer for forward-looking information also tends to appear in this section, although not all companies in our sample included it. The formal financial statements tend to appear toward the end of the report. The associated notes follow them. These sections principally provide mandated information and disclosures. They provide historical data and are primarily concerned with financial matters. Reports usually conclude with a page or two of information for shareholders, often including more information about stock price performance.

Two elements of annual reports that might appear anywhere are information about the board of directors and multiyear selected financial information comparisons (showing up to 10 or more years of historical information). Companies vary on disclosing background information of board members and of board activities. Key officers' contributions to the company are sometimes discussed elsewhere in the report, but most companies report only the names and titles of key officers in this section.

Orientation

Annual reports are constructed to address the information needs of many groups, and the orientation of the reports (toward analysts, individual investors, or customers) varies. While there are clearly efforts to communicate to a variety of users, companies differ in both the principal orientation and the pervasiveness of the principal orientation. Some seem principally oriented toward single classes of users, while others seem oriented toward multiple classes. To the extent that reports are oriented toward single classes of users, we found several styles of reports, including those focusing on communicating with sophisticated investors and analysts, those focusing on customers, those focusing on the communities in which the company operates, and those focusing on individual investors.

The variations in the focus on the particular needs of some users can be inferred from the annual report focus and content. Detailed specialized and proprietary information is of interest to financial analysts and institutional investors. This constituency also benefits from very detailed information at the business line, segment, and product level that often includes profitability, sales, and cost information. An orientation toward individual investors, both current and potential, is indicated by annual reports that have strong themes, substantial use of graphics and images, broad discussions of the company's major lines of business and its commitment to excellence, and investment return prospects. Our sample suggests that many annual reports are strongly oriented toward the relatively unsophisticated investor, because they tend to introduce the company in ways that presume little prior knowledge or specialized training.

Annual reports are not only for investors. They are often constructed to be useful to other groups, even when their principal orientation is toward investors. Furthermore, some companies appear to orient their reporting toward potential customers by emphasizing the advantage offered by doing business with the company. This also results in a deemphasis of the financial accounting component of the reports. Some firms are more mindful than others of groups such as employees, community advocates, and government regulators. In selected companies, deference to these interests seems to have influenced the content of annual reports. It seems plausible to conjecture that such orientations reflect particular concerns of companies. For example, a company concerned about its image in the communities in which it operates might include elements in its annual report to address that issue.

1992/1997 Comparison

The years 1992 and 1997 were chosen more for the interval between them than for any particular characteristics of these years. At the onset of this project, 1997 year-ends provided the most recent annual reports, and 1992 provided a five-year comparison period. Comparisons between 1992 and 1997 for each of the companies leads to the insight that company annual reporting is highly distinctive. Thus, a simple general observation of the annual reports cannot be formed. It cannot be said, for example, that the 1997 annual reports invariably contain more nonfinancial information than the 1992 reports, or that they contain substantially less. Rather, annual reports are documents whose content and format are contingent on company culture, management, products, performance, regulatory requirements, and a variety of other factors.

Nonetheless, numerous observations are worth noting. In terms of firm complexity, an interesting dichotomy is observed. Firms that became less complex between 1992 and 1997—for example, following a spin-off of a major part of the company—usually have a 1997 report that contains less total information. Presumably, less complex firms have less information to present, and the companies observed do not correspondingly increase the depth of disclosures about the rest of the company. Thus, when firms become less complex, the total amount of information in the second report may decrease. However, this does not mean that the report is less informative. Instead, it should be interpreted as a communication from a distinctly less complex entity.

In contrast, there is little evidence in the sample that firms that become more complex as the result of an acquisition or merger report more information. An increase in complexity does not tend to translate into a proportionately longer or more detailed report. This means that less information about continuing operations results, as some attention is transferred to the new operations. In sum, changes in the composition of the company will affect the composition of the annual report, but it is difficult to predict exactly how the report will be affected. Several of the firms in our sample were involved in such transitions, and the 1992/1997 comparisons reflect these fundamental changes.

It is plausible to conjecture that the comparison of these two years might be clouded by the changing profitability of the companies. However, we observe no systematic difference between the amount of disclosure that companies make following profitable years and years when losses occur. Our sample includes a wide range of profitability and profitability changes. For example, some companies earned record profits in the two years, some recorded increases in profitability, and others recorded decreases in profitability.

While profitability does not affect overall disclosure level, it does seem to affect the composition of disclosures. In loss years, management tends to focus on improving performance. Accordingly, a more pronounced future orientation is evident when corporate profitability is low.

Several sample companies experienced changes in top management between 1992 and 1997. Assuming that the annual report is a unique expression by the top managers of a company, stylistic and content changes would be expected in these companies. For the most part, there is no evidence of such changes. While there are exceptions, annual reports are generally quite similar in both years, and differences that do appear do not seem to be associated with changes in management.

Every year, designers of annual reports face many choices. One is the trade-off between depth of coverage and breadth of coverage. The annual report is not infinitely expandable, so it is difficult to increase both. Between 1992 and 1997, there does not seem to be a distinct trend in either direction. In both years, the average number of pages in an annual report is 55. Companies must also decide whether to tell more about themselves or to provide more information about their operating and economic environment—market, industry, competitors, and so forth. The latter may be important to the extent that the performance of the company depends on its environment. There does seem to be a trend toward more of this type of information in the annual reports of 1997. Annual reports are becoming venues, for example, for important industry analysis, because they provide information about the beliefs of key participants.

Another issue pertains to reporting the results for the entire company versus reporting results for segments. Segments themselves can be divided into product lines. Product lines can then be analyzed geographically. Thus, a number of levels are suggested that can be traversed in terms of information disaggregation. There appears to be somewhat greater production of information about individual segments and about individual products in 1997, perhaps reflecting the pending implementation of SFAS 131. Although this observation has exceptions, readers of annual reports in 1997 appear to be getting a closer look at more detailed information for companies than those in 1992. Much of the information is selective, unsystematic, and nonquantified. In fact, no general trend toward quantitative information is observed over this time period, and unique metrics such as free cash flow measures are not extended into the segment levels.

In addition to studying change in the substance of communication, we studied annual report formats, as mentioned above. Companies may differ in how they communicate as well as what they communicate. While modern finance theory suggests that format is unimportant, it is important if it affects how information is understood and the likelihood that information will be considered. The reports studied reveal some departures from the stereotypical format. Such departures may help make a company's annual report and message memorable to the extent that other companies' annual reports have become so crystallized and stolid in design and style that they are ineffective at communicating with their constituents. If magazine- and catalog-style annual reports, which are more evident in 1997, are better at communicating with a company's constituents, the fact that they may appear untraditional and differently informative may be an acceptable, and even desirable, trade-off.

The study also notes use of the "summary annual report." These reports contain less than a full set of accounting information, such that the annual report must be combined with a supplemental document to provide a full set of mandated information. This alternative might be viewed as a model for communicating nonfinancial, nonmandated information. The two instances in the sample both appeared in 1997, and it is unclear whether these are isolated cases or evidence of a trend. In one case nontraditional information is plentiful, and in the other it is minimal.

Other changes between 1992 and 1997 include a slight trend to more graphics and other non-narrative presentation forms. Pictures have also become more purposeful and innovative and less likely to fall into the smiling employee or pure product shot categories. Customers are making more photographic appearances in annual reports.

The 1997 reports make some forays into novel areas, some of which have not been thoroughly studied before. Key among these are future-oriented materials. Reports are including more future-oriented material, though forward-looking predictions (such as specific earnings forecasts) are still infrequent. By 1997, most annual reports say something about the company's prospects going forward, whereas this orientation was less prominent and general in 1992. Again, however, this information is unsystematic, selective, and not quantified.

Annual reports in 1997 are less likely to be documents produced by U.S.-based companies discussing U.S. business. Instead, they are chronicles of progressive globalization. Companies that have had a fully globalized business for some time are now beginning to produce annual reports that reflect their geographic dispersion.

Finally, more content in the area of social responsibility can be observed in the 1997 reports in terms of ethicality, environmentalism, community involvement, and charitable contributions.

Future-oriented/Forward-looking Information

There is a considerable amount of information about the future in the annual reports examined. Critics of corporate communications who assert that annual reports contain only historical information are incorrect. This study identifies two types of such information: future-oriented and forward-looking information. Future-oriented information (as discussed above) is "softer" information that helps readers assess the future prospects of a company by understanding its strategies, production, products (including new and in-development products), and expansion plans. This information is generally not quantified, nor does it represent a specific forecast. Future-oriented information is ubiquitous in annual reports. In contrast, forward-looking information is composed of specific forecasts and predictions, typically quantified, made by a company and covered under the forward-looking safe harbor provisions of the Securities and Exchange Commission (SEC).

Future-oriented or forward-looking information tends to be idiosyncratic and relatively unique to the company that offers it. This is logical, because every company faces a different future dominated by a special set of critical success factors. Nonetheless, it can be understood in juxtaposition with the required content of corporate communication. In this way, judgments about its relevance or value are not necessary.

Some of the forward-looking information items in the annual reports are linear extensions of existing accounting information. For example, prices for the company's products are projected and future costs are anticipated. Along similar lines, companies that describe how cash will be used in the short term provide information closely connected to the traditional accounting paradigm.

A group of other future-oriented disclosures pertains to the factors of production. These represent a departure from the traditional accounting model. Examples are commentary on expected productive capacity and changes in the levels of the future workforce. Because government is able to sharply limit what can take place in the private sector, the discussion of anticipated changes in regulatory policy also fits into this category.

Another level of future-oriented information is information about new products. This represents a kind of lateral expression of accounting information, since it pertains potentially to new markets, new customers, and progressively deepening market power. Included as new product information are data on product performance, processes used to develop new products, and the continuing viability of older products. Sharing this level is information about the progressive globalization of the enterprise. Like new products, globalization expands the reach of the company in ways that should enhance accounting numbers such as sales, cash flow, and profit. When a company reports breakthroughs on international fronts, it signals important information about future possibilities.

Several companies announce performance targets. Most of these targets pertain to profitability, although targets may also be specified for debt reduction or dividend payments. Although these targets also involve future accounting numbers, they are qualitatively different in that they relate to the prospects of the entire company and are explicit expectations. These embedded plans for the future extend well beyond traditional accounting information. Similar to stated profit percentages are target market shares and growth levels expected for particular parts of the organization.

Farther afield, some future-oriented statements pertain to relationships with other organizations and, therefore, relate to the nature of the company in the future. For example, some firms talk about evolving partnerships with their customers. Several others announce priorities that would bring about a much different entity over time.

Most statements made by these corporations about their culture, their leadership, and their innovativeness can be viewed as descriptive of current conditions. However, if they really pertain to distinctive advantages, their elaboration in annual reports amounts to a future-oriented statement. If a firm has strong culture, industry leadership, and systematic innovativeness, these characteristics should continue to benefit the company in many ways that ultimately translate into superior profitability and growth. However, rhetorical claims about these matters often do not include what most would consider verifiable information. The tendency for future-oriented information to be qualitative can be compared with historical information, which is more often quantitative.

COMPANY PROFILES

This section summarizes our assessments of each of the 16 companies studied. Companies have individual histories, relationships, industries, management, corporate ownership structure, and other characteristics. Accordingly, no two annual reports can be expected to be identical in content or scope, and the nonmandated components of annual reports, in particular, vary widely. Consequently, we employed a case study method to analyze the content of individual annual reports. Our analysis focuses on describing individual companies, although some comparative data are presented where warranted.

The individual company profiles are organized using the following set of categories: overall impression, level of detail, relatively unique content, structure of the reports, target audiences or orientation, 1992/1997 comparison, and future-oriented/forward-looking materials. These categories collectively summarize the content of the annual reports and the information items found there.

We begin by providing an overall impression that summarizes our general insights regarding the company's annual report. Presumably, companies design annual reports to portray important aspects and convey fundamental messages about themselves, and we attempt to capture this aspect of the reports in our overall impression. This overall impression reflects the entire content of the report, including its pictures and the subject matter of its discretionary narratives, and the content and tone of the CEO's letter.

Next we summarize the level of detail in a company's reports. Level of detail refers to both the overall volume of informative details and the level of information disaggregation. Then we discuss the notable and unique content or presentation format found in a company's reports. We use the term "unique" to mean noteworthy, distinctive, innovative, or notable disclosures. Therefore, uniqueness, as we use the term, is relative, and should not be interpreted as implying singularity. Each annual report has innovative content. Often, the information spotlighted in this section for a particular company stands out as the only representative of its kind in this sample. Notable content or format may reflect performance measures, other interesting and unusual content, or innovative ways of presenting information.

Our summary then describes the organization of each company's annual reports. While there are some similarities across the reports, in part related to regulatory requirements, the reports are also quite different in structure. Often a single company's reports are different between years. This section amplifies and describes in detail the information quantified in table 3.

We also considered the target audiences or orientation of the reports. In general, an annual report might be oriented to meet the information needs of or convey important messages to individual investors, institutional investors and analysts, creditors, employees, customers, or communities. Furthermore, different parts of reports may be oriented to different audiences. While this is always a matter of degree, the fact that there are different constituents or stakeholders with varying information needs and limited company resources for preparing an annual report suggests that companies must choose the target audiences for their reports.

Next we compared each company's annual reports (1992 and 1997). Our primary work in this area involved comparisons of categories and types of information reported, as well as differences in structure, detail, and orientation. In the summary of the two years, new content in the latter year and missing content in the latter year were both considered.

The final element of the company profiles is a special evaluation of future-oriented and forward-looking information. Although the historic function of the annual report has been to report on the results of the previous year, an increasingly important task has been to establish realistic expectations about the future. Forward-looking information consists of disclosures involving explicit forecasts and estimates of future performance. In contrast, future-oriented information is more general, dealing with aspects of the company's operations that will bear on its future performance, such as new or in-development products, changes in strategies, and company restructuring or refocusing activities. This section summarizes the extent to which annual reports contain such information.

1

Champion International Corporation

Overview

Champion International represents the annual reports of a company in a challenging economic environment. The company reports losses in both 1992 and 1997. These losses were not typical of company performance, because the company reported profits in the intervening years, and the 1992 loss was attributable to the adoption of accounting standards. The dominant theme of the related communication is the difficulty of establishing proactive management in an economic situation beyond the company's control. The reports are constructed to focus attention on production issues rather than on the sales environment. Champion portrays itself as a company seeking to improve its efficiency, for example in terms of extracting more wood product outputs from a given amount of inputs. This is consistent with the cover of the 1992 report, which shows an upward-sloping graph of the company's productivity growth. While both reports provide an adequate picture of past results, their principal focus is on future prospects. Accordingly, we observe a high level of future-oriented and forward-looking information, primarily related to expectation of more favorable prices for the company's products.

Level of Detail

In addition to forward-looking and future-oriented information, Champion provides a high level of detail about the pricing structures in its markets. This often includes past, current, and expected future prices, and even "what if" prices. The reader of these reports also receives a view of the company's productive processes. The critical factors of success for a wood products company are presented as productive efficiency issues.

Relatively Unique Content

Several pieces of information that are not typical of our sample appear in the Champion annual reports. In addition to considerable use of physical volume metrics to describe production, Champion provides information comparing actual production (by major market sector) with total capacity. A reader would deduce the importance of operating the company's mills at or near full capacity in restoring company profitability. This provides an opportunity to consider the efficiency of use of corporate facilities. In addition, the 1992 report references specialized productivity measures. Activity level and asset size denominators attest to rising productivity.

Structure of the Reports

In both 1992 and 1997, the Champion report begins with one or two pages of introductory text. The 1992 material celebrates the 100th year of operations with information about the company's size and productivity. The 1997 report's introduction focuses on the strategies at work in the company's major product lines. To further this sense, it creates a "1997 Timeline of Strategic Events" for these pages. Both reports offer a general CEO's letter. The 1997 letter opens with a full-page close-up picture of the CEO's face, accompanied by text suggesting that he will answer all questions. The 1997 report prefaces the letter with a full-page quote from the CEO's letter. In fact, portraits (1997) and full-page quotes (1992) are used throughout as a way to transition to new sections. Although different CEOs wrote the letters, they share a focus on the industry and the broader economic climate, with ample attention to future-oriented information. The CEO's letter in 1997 indicates this theme with "Focusing on Strategic Businesses," "Increasing Profitability," and "Improving Financial Discipline" sections. A summary of performance and prospects in each of the company's markets follows. This narrative is divided by major product lines (nine in 1992, five in 1997).

The 1992 review also includes sections for its major subsidiaries and for its export activities. The 1997 review is broken up with full-page testimonials from employees and shareholders, each answering a question about Champion's direction and values.

Supplemental financial information follows in a section called "Financial Review" in 1992 and "Financial Highlights" in 1997. In addition to total company information, accounting information is provided on a disaggregated basis. In 1997, ongoing and divestiture totals are distinguished, with some information further disaggregated by product types within larger divisions. Time-series data are presented graphically (bar charts) and show recent historical comparisons among price, production, and capacity. The next section contains the full financial statements and associated notes. MD&A follows, with a higher level of textual detail. This section is organized topically within two general sections, "Results of Operations" and "Financial Condition," and is sometimes further subdivided by product line. A sizable part of each MD&A section is concerned with environmental matters. The reports conclude with the names of board members and key officers. In both years, a description of the function of the board committees (and their members) is provided.

Orientation

The annual report of Champion appears to be principally oriented toward existing shareholders. For instance, immediately following the CEO's letter in the 1997 report is a full-page picture of the managing director of Oppenheimer Capital answering the question, "Why Should I Invest in Champion?"

1992/1997 Comparison

By 1997, leadership at Champion International has changed with the retirement and replacement of the chairman and CEO in 1996. In the 1997 report the company discusses its plans to divest several of its principal businesses. Whereas the penetration of new markets was an often-referenced aspect of the 1992 report, the focus of efforts on more selective core areas came through as the message of the 1997 report. The theme of the 1997 report, "A Different Champion," reflects the divestiture of several business lines that the 1992 report projected as promising. Notably, although the company is more focused in 1997, its annual report is neither shorter nor less complex. With some exceptions, the distribution of information items was remarkably similar over the two periods. Considering that there are fewer lines of business in 1997, the amount of company information in the 1997 report is relatively larger than in 1992. The 1997 report also reflects a stronger concern with the cost of regulatory (environmental) compliance. The 1992 report presents a more precise and detailed discussion of specific price movements.

Future-oriented/Forward-looking Information

Each component of these reports concerns itself with information such as expected future prices, anticipated production levels at specific facilities, and the expected completion dates for new factories and distribution centers. The reports also identify firm assets that are to be sold in the near future. Substantial specificity is provided in areas such as expected environmental compliance expenditure, anticipated workforce reductions, and expected changes in product demand. Performance targets are often quantified. The company communicates the seriousness of its efforts to improve productivity and to aggressively contain costs. It also implies that its strategy will result in a considerable payoff when prices recover, enabling the company to be restored to record profitability.

2

The Coca-Cola Company

Overview

Coca-Cola highlights its global mission in its annual reports. The reports also provide detailed information about its worldwide efforts to capture the beverage market. This company presents itself as very focused and highly successful in its industry, with goals of continuing its levels of achievement and industry leadership. The reports portray the intricacies of the relationships between the Coca-Cola Company and its many bottling affiliates across the world. The 1992 report includes an evaluation of the company's positioning to capitalize on investment opportunities; and both annual reports detail the extent to which the company believes that it has accomplished these goals.

Level of Detail

Most of the detail Coca-Cola provides pertains to the relative success of its efforts to sell product in many different countries and regions. The annual reports disclose sales in nearly 200 different countries or regions. A relatively high level of detail also exists for the company's estimates of total market size. For example, the company discusses cities in the United States with the highest and lowest per capita Coca-Cola consumption. Some product-specific data are presented, sometimes also reported by geographic area. At 74 and 68 pages, respectively, the 1992 and 1997 Coca-Cola annual reports have ample room for the considerable detail that they offer. The detail the Coca-Cola Company achieves in its reports is noteworthy, given its relatively narrow product line.

Relatively Unique Content

Coca-Cola's metric "total cases shipped" pervades the reports and serves as notable content. This translates into the idea that volume statistics are important in the management of this company. Growth is sought in bottlers' unit case volume, which drives gallon shipments of product concentrate. Another unique piece of information is the per capita consumption figures. The theme of the 1997 report, "One Billion Servings Per Day," is quite consistent with this measure in its recitation of an ambitious goal that was recently achieved. When combined with the remainder of the message, "47 billion to go," the report reemphasizes the demographic-driven growth agenda of the company. Per capita company sales numbers are often juxtaposed with per capita beverage consumption (including drinking water). In this way, Coca-Cola makes it clear that it sees every person in the world as a potential customer and that it is interested in its total market share objective. The focus on worldwide population demographics and potential cola market is also typified by the 1992 theme "New Worlds of Opportunity."

Structure of the Reports

The 1992 and 1997 reports are similarly structured. This similarity is noteworthy in light of the fact that there were a number of different members of the management team in 1997. Following financial highlights, a brief CEO's letter that hits the top performance highlights is provided. This letter is followed by a lengthy review of operations section that contains much of the essential information in the reports. This section is organized primarily by geographic region. This structure allows for a discussion of the potential of each area and the relative success of current market penetration. It also serves, in both years, to remind the reader in no uncertain terms that the company possesses some of the world's most recognizable (and most valuable) brands, and that it maximizes shareholder value by a relentless desire for growth. The next section is MD&A, which provides a more standard content and focuses more on the company as a whole than do previous sections. The financial statements amplified by the MD&A make it clear that the firm's fundamental financial strength is its ability to generate cash in excess of its reinvestment and dividend requirements. The MD&A section is not as detailed as the preceding section. Financial statements and associated notes come next. The latter contain more than the usual amount of incremental information. The materials at the end of the reports include information about the board of directors and information pertaining to share prices, a glossary, and access information addressed to shareholders.

Orientation

The pervasive growth orientation and disclosure detail of the Coca-Cola annual reports suggests that the intended audiences are analysts and institutional investors. The company's extensive use of metrics such as economic profit and economic value added further establishes its sophisticated approach to performance measurement. The use of the "cases of concentrate shipped" measure makes it possible to assess the company's attainment of its objectives. The reports are also oriented toward shareholders and consumers, generally. The reports adopt a playful spirit, particularly around the idea of refreshment. There is considerable polish in the reports, specifically in the use of photography and portraits of average Coca-Cola drinkers in colorful and exotic geographical backdrops. This creates an equally important orientation toward individual shareholders and current owners. The company adds a glossary of technical terms at the end of both of the reports to make it more user-friendly.

1992/1997 Comparison

In most respects, the two Coca-Cola reports are similar. Both orient themselves around physical measures and are forthright about their conceptions of the market and their place as the dominant player within it. The 1997 report contains more information about acquisitions since it reflects a new strategy to proactively deal in this way with its bottling partners. The 1992 report is more focused on the company's short- and long-term objectives at the geographical business level. The 1997 report provides more information about advertising campaigns and other attempts to promote products. The 1992 report dwells more on industry conditions. Both the 1992 and 1997 reports are sales and market-share oriented. Neither report has much information about costs, production, or the many nonsales aspects of the company. The 1997 report identifies the development of employees' skills and learning as a core capacity and provides greater clarity about the company's fundamental financial ability to generate cash from operations in excess of capital reinvestment and dividend needs.

Future-oriented/Forward-looking Information

The 1992 annual report of Coca-Cola provides clear statements about expected market share and the sales potential of certain markets. The company emphasizes estimates of trends in beverage consumption. For example, it cites a trend to sweet/cold beverages in nations currently dominated by tea consumption as its own sweet/cold beverages become more available. This information juxtaposes demographic and current sales data and, accordingly, becomes forward-looking information by implicitly inviting the reader to project growth rates for the company's products, both within a region and across regions.

Other future-oriented information is limited. In 1992, Coca-Cola announced plans for a $1 billion investment in overseas production plants and distribution centers to be completed by 1995. In 1997, a plan to reduce the target dividend payout ratio from 34 percent to 30 percent was announced. The 1997 report suggests a forward-looking intention to attempt to raise funds at lower cost through strategic debt-management programs.

The particular division of responsibility between Coca-Cola and its bottling partners may make future-oriented statements about developing infrastructure unnecessary. Currently, the company's focus is on finding appropriate bottling partners and ensuring their performance. The dependence of the company on successful advertising, even outside the United States, is not made explicit in the annual reports. By focusing on population demographics, the reports suggest a certain inevitability to increased worldwide demand that is independent of advertising. As stated by the chairman in the 1997 report, Coca-Cola offers value via "a simple moment of refreshment and good times." Overall, the most basic future orientation of the company as presented in its annual reports is the strategy of convincing the world's residents of the desirability of Coca-Cola products.

3

ConAgra, Inc.

Overview

The annual reports of ConAgra describe a diversified food manufacturing and distributing company. To quote the company, ConAgra operates "across the food chain." This phrase, meant to imply the breadth of its product offerings, also creates a spirit that permeates its annual reports. The annual reports provide a detailed look at the multiple markets in which the company participates, most of which converge in supermarket sales. Particular strengths include its descriptions of the challenges for product market share and the importance of satisfying consumer demand. The 1992 report is based on a "Strong Foundation, New Dimensions" theme that emphasizes expanding product lines. The 1997 report uses "An Appetite for Excellence" theme that features existing strong offerings. Both themes emphasize products.

Level of Detail

The trade-off of breadth for depth made by a company as complex as ConAgra results in an array of information. Mostly taken up with the relative performance of specific divisions, segments, and product lines, ConAgra's reports provide a great deal of detail. A portion of this information is presented by segment, in the coding forms approaching nearly half of all the informational items found. The company also provides extensive information about its products (e.g., increased distribution of particular products in the retail market) and industry information (e.g., effects of the Asian economic crisis and domestic protein supply on demand for pork).

ConAgra provides information about specific product lines and, occasionally, some indication of associated operational issues. For example, in the 1997 report, there are numerous references to change in management in some food divisions, which appear to be related to prior results. These announcements also convey an implicit message about how the company responds to performance disappointments. Overall, similar amounts of operational information were disclosed in both 1992 and 1997. Although ConAgra does business around the world, the reporting focus is product markets; therefore, relatively less explicit attention is paid to geographic segments. The reports do include international operations as a reportable segment in the MD&A, where the focus of discretionary narratives is toward products. The 1997 report demonstrates an increased emphasis on geographic disclosure, containing maps with locations of company operations. Given the magnitude of ConAgra's business, more detail in any particular area would greatly increase the size of the report, which is 54 and 74 pages for fiscal years 1992 and 1997, respectively.

Relatively Unique Content

ConAgra focuses on the concept of "cash earnings" as its preferred performance indicator. The company uses a net income plus amortization calculation that is familiar to analysts. This is ConAgra's definition of earnings available to the business for growth and dividends. This measure is reported for the firm overall, rather than permeating the segment or product line information. The firm also measures overall performance against a target trend line objective. Again, this is reported only at the company level. For other levels of operations, ConAgra discusses performance measures that are common with many other companies—it seeks volume increases and profitability enhancements. These performance measures are usually denominated in percentage terms using the previous year as the baseline. The sheer number of these data, often in progressively smaller product market niches, constitutes notable content in the ConAgra reports.

Structure of the Reports

The 1992 and 1997 reports are similar in structure. After a few pages of introductory material (e.g., financial highlights, pictures), a brief CEO's letter, touching on important aspects of operations, is provided. This letter is followed by a two-page section entitled "Objectives and Results," providing current and historical overview performance data. A focus of this section is to relate achieved performance to the internal targets established by the company. The bulk of the detailed information is in the next section, entitled "Business Review." This section provides discussions of the reportable food group segments and various product lines within the segments. In 1992 and 1997, these major divisions include classes of products such as prepared foods, refrigerated foods, and shelf-stable foods. The 1997 report shows a more complex arrangement. In addition to some sections organized around product classes, other sections pertain to the company's objectives for its products, such as convenience and product safety, and still others provide categorization by company attributes, such as innovation and "working smarter." The MD&A section focuses on overall company results, referring the reader to the previous segment discussion for more details. ConAgra provides an 11-year time series of key financial data items. Typical board/executives, facilities, and shareholder/investor relations information sections appear at the end of the reports, following the audited financial statements and notes thereto.

Orientation

ConAgra's reports are focused on its brand identities. They are filled with qualitative detail and include a few quantitative items about each segment, such as sales and profitability. An analyst who specializes in the food industry (or one of its many subsets) should find information such as the number of acres the company has planted in soybeans or that a particular brand is a "best volume performer" helpful to the process of learning about the overall environment for this company. An analyst who has been tracking ConAgra for a while could also piece together some information about how specific divisions of the company are performing, both absolutely and in relation to previous performance. The development of detailed quantitative information would require an analyst to have been tracking this company over a long period. The aspect of the reports that would appeal to the individual investor is the constant parade of recognizable brand names, but the contents of ConAgra's annual report do not appear to be directed to such parties. Nonetheless, an individual would be favorably impressed that a single firm sells so many familiar food products.

1992/1997 Comparison

The 1997 annual report of ConAgra represents an elaboration of the 1992 annual report. This difference could be merely the result of the more complicated company that had emerged by 1997. For example, by 1997 ConAgra had many more product lines and variations within product lines to discuss. Each of these new products had volume changes, price changes, and profitability changes that could be mentioned. The 1992–1997 period saw a proliferation of variety (e.g., low fat, low sodium) as the company sought to capture increasingly compartmentalized sectors of the overall grocery store food demand. The two reports are similarly structured and there are no significant changes with respect to the company mission or strategy, perhaps owing to the nature of the industry. Product photography, both large full-page and small margin shots, pervades the reports. The 1997 report engages in more of the former. This explains, in part, the considerable expansion in length in 1997.

Future-oriented/Forward-looking Information

This company provides qualitative and future-oriented, but usually not quantitative, forward-looking information. Future-oriented information in the ConAgra reports tends to concentrate in two areas. First, plans for new products to be developed are readily provided. This gives insight into where new development can be made and allows the reader to assess the products' market potential. Second, expected increases in productive capacity are mentioned with some frequency. ConAgra does provide forward-looking information in terms of target profit, debt, and dividends for the entire firm. The company portrays its confidence, in both years, in its ability to achieve an aggregate earnings trend line and its dividend payment trend. Similar information at less aggregated levels is not provided. In 1997, ConAgra includes a forward-looking information disclaimer, but discloses a similar amount of forward-looking and future-oriented information to that disclosed in 1992.

Dell Computer Corporation

Overview

Dell Computer Corporation uses a unique approach to sell a technologically sophisticated product line to a diverse group of customers. The company has enjoyed exceptional growth and profitability in the 1990s and has become a market leader in several product areas. Dell's annual reports portray a company that has carefully developed and mastered unique methods of marketing, manufacturing, selling, and servicing its products—its "direct business model." In the 1992 annual report, the company focuses on the implementation of this strategy with its retail consumer customer group. The report's narratives provide substantial details about many aspects of the company's operations, and it uses benchmarks to compare itself with both its own previous performance and the performance of other companies in the computer industry. The 1997 report contains even more of this benchmarking. The 1997 report places less emphasis on specific products and operational details, but continues to stress the company's strategy, its international growth, and the usefulness of its products to its customers. Dell's annual reports reflect the company's need to differentiate itself in a dynamic, competitive marketplace.

Level of Detail

The annual report of Dell Corporation grew from 42 pages in 1992 to 54 pages in 1997; however, the earlier report contains substantially more detailed descriptions of the company's operations. There were a number of disclosures about hedging activities, forward-looking statements, and related discussions of company risks as well as opportunities in the 1992 report. In both reports, several pages (6 in 1992, 13 in 1997) consist almost entirely of images, and contain little or no text.

Even though the 1992 report focuses extensively on Dell's relationships with its suppliers and customers, it also contains a large amount of operational, financial, and product detail. The 1997 report, in contrast, is less detailed in this way. Instead, the company discusses its financial position, marketing, and product/service offerings at a more strategic level. By 1997, the development of the computer industry may have led the company to look beyond the detailed focus on the performance of particular products.

Relatively Unique Content

Dell's annual reports benchmark the company's condition and performance extensively, in terms of both year-to-year comparisons and comparisons against industry averages. The attention that computers have received in the media in the past few years has led to a considerable external focus on product performance. The inclusion of this information, in the form of various third-party rankings in the 1997 report, provides support for the product claims made by management. Both reports provide some information on specific customers, but the 1997 report includes mini-case studies of how several customers used Dell's products or services. These cases highlight individual customers, their "situation," the "solution" provided by Dell products, and the corresponding "benefits" generated by the customer.

Additional unique content that appears in the 1992 report is detailed narrative discussions of Dell's operations, including the company's outlook and its hedging activities. It also discusses in depth an ongoing SEC inquiry into appropriate accounting for such transactions, revealing the general contours of the debate about applicable reporting standards. Throughout, Dell provides what appears to be a frank assessment of the opportunities and risks it faces, and the critical elements necessary for Dell to continue its record of growth and profitability.

The company benchmarks itself using a variety of year-to-year and industry measures, including market share, competitive position, return on invested capital, inventories, and common stock performance and returns.

Structure of the Reports

In both years, Dell's reports begin with a few pages of performance highlights. These are followed by the CEO's letter, which contains many of the performance benchmarks. Both reports insert performance graphs of several types in the borders of the letter. The next section, titled "Year in Review" in 1992 and untitled in 1997, presents an overview of the company's activities. This section consists of 10 pages in 1992 and 20 in 1997, but the 1997 report contains more photo-only pages. Customer mini-cases, featuring the application of Dell products used by major companies, are summarized in the 1997 report. The 1992 textual materials are far more detailed and extensive. In the 1992 report, this section discusses many aspects of the company's operations and strategies. The 1992 report then presents a page of "selected consolidated financial data" before an eight-page MD&A section. Like the "Year in Review," the MD&A section contains substantial, detailed analysis of the company. The financial statements and notes are followed by a page that lists directors and officers and a page of stockholder information. The notes to the financial statements contain some supplemental financial information in the form of more detailed breakdowns of line items on the balance sheet and income statement. The customer mini-cases are interspersed throughout this section, and the report contains more pages that are principally graphics. The five-page MD&A in the 1997 report is less detailed. The notes to the financial statements again contain some supplemental financial information, similar to the same section in the 1992 report. The 1997 report also concludes with a page of officers and directors and a page of investor information.

Orientation

Dell's 1992 report has extensive narratives filled with operational and strategic detail. This information seems most likely to be valuable to a sophisticated investor. The 1997 report actually increases the use of benchmark statistics, but the extensive textual detail is substantially reduced, and so is the informativeness of the report to such an investor. The 1997 report seems to be designed to appeal to potential customers. The increased substance and space devoted to the customer mini-cases is similar to marketing efforts that would appear in places other than the annual report.

1992/1997 Comparison

Where the 1992 annual report contains extensive narrative details and limited graphics, the 1997 report contains more graphical and effects-oriented pages. Devoting entire pages (and substantial white space) to the customer mini-cases renders the 1997 report more anecdotal. Whereas the 1992 report focuses on the characteristics of the products being sold or developed by the company (particularly its new products), the 1997 report is written at a much broader strategic level, focusing more on the direction of the company. Overall, the 1992 report is focused on the operational level, while the 1997 report is focused on the strategic level.

The period between 1992 and 1997 saw considerable technological progress in computers. The 1997 report focuses far less on technological issues, perhaps driven by these rapidly changing technologies. Instead, Dell's 1997 report focuses on its comparative marketing and sales strengths with a corresponding increase in details about corporate customers' use of Dell products. The 1992 report also contains some unique content related to forward-looking statements and the company's hedging activities, not present in the 1997 report. This difference may reflect a change in the company's use of certain financial instruments as a risk-reducing device.

Future-oriented/Forward-looking Information

Dell provides some forward-looking and future-oriented information in both reports, but more are presented in 1992 than in 1997. In both years, most forward-looking and future-oriented information appears in the MD&A section of the reports and principally relates to the overall outlook for the company. This information is infrequently quantified. The 1992 report contains a number of specific performance and strategy predictions, but also includes numerous disclaimers of those predictions. The MD&A section in 1997 also includes a few mostly qualitative predictions, but the individual disclaimers are not included.

5

The Dow Chemical Company

Overview

Dow presents itself in its annual reports as a strong, successful, established company facing only partially controllable markets. In its 1992 report, Dow conveys a message that its markets are unpredictable and difficult to control. Its position in 1997 is more proactive. The company's general theme in both years is its efforts to renew and reinvigorate itself. In the two years examined, Dow appears to be evolving from a company that conceives of itself as a singular business to that of a company that possesses a portfolio of businesses. The latter perspective entails a greater attention to merger and acquisition possibilities and a greater openness to changing the fundamental nature of the business in the future.

Level of Detail

A substantial amount of detailed information is contained in Dow's reports, principally in MD&A. Frequently, the reports elaborate on required disclosures that could be meaningful to those interested in Dow. The information in Dow's reports is often organized around its products as they fit within the business activity structure that is identified in the reports. In 1997, the company used a balanced business portfolio presentation. Although the volume of detail varied across the two years, productive capacity and market outlook were areas of concentration for both. The company provides ample business-level detail, also mostly in the MD&A section of each report. Dow does not seem to provide information aimed at marketing its products.

Relatively Unique Content

Dow, in 1992, states its strategic decisions to accrue certain costs. Dow also has an unusually extensive environmental discussion, perhaps at least partly attributable to the nature of its business. The amount of this content, both from the remediation/prevention and the cost/accrual perspectives, should be considered unique. Finally, a mention of Dow's mandatory retirement age in the 1992 report stands out as an unusual piece of information.

Structure of the Reports

With some key differences, Dow's two reports have a similar structure. In both years, the reports are noteworthy for providing significant content without being repetitive. The reports refer the reader to other pages for detail or more information, rather than repeating the information in two places. Both reports begin with introductory material. The 1992 report confines itself to financial highlights. The 1997 introduction is more diffuse, with more company profile information. Whereas the 1992 introduction tells how the company performed, the 1997 introduction tells what the company is, where it makes its money, and where it is going. The next section in both reports is the CEO's letter to shareholders. Both letters are summaries of the report, although the 1997 letter provides a table of portfolio changes over the previous year. The 1997 letter is twice as long as the 1992 letter. Instead of building detail into the CEO's letter, the 1992 report offers a special section immediately following the letter that summarizes significant corporate changes over the previous four years. The next section in both reports is a narrative, divided into subtopics. The 1992 subtopics are "Competitiveness," "Changing Needs," "Technology," "Global Marketplace Issues," and "Environmental Investments." The 1997 subtopics are "Depth: Product and Technology Pipeline," "Range: Growth in New Markets," and "Dimension: Sharing Success with All Stakeholders." Despite these differing packages, the content and purpose of these narrative sections are similar. The length of the material is also comparable over the two years. The MD&A section comes next. This section includes a "Market Outlook" for each of the company's segments. Although the identity of the segments is different in 1992 and 1997, the basic template for reporting is similar. This similarity is also indicated by the number of pages (11 in 1992 and 12 in 1997). The financial statement, complete with the associated notes, appears next, followed by an 11-year performance summary. This summary includes stock price data and an unaudited product sales analysis in both years. The report concludes with information about the board of directors and organizational information about the company.

Orientation

Dow's reporting has the depth of analysis and the magnitude of detailed information to be suitable for analysts and institutional investors, who may be able to use the details to track activities over time. At the same time, the way Dow uses the report to tell its recent history, to relate its current positioning, and to illustrate its strategy of moving forward suggests a broader orientation. The reports would be valuable to new investors as a way of acquainting themselves with Dow. Prospective employees might also benefit from such a detailed picture of the company's operations.

1992/1997 Comparison

The basic format of the two reports is the same. However, the tone of the discussions changes somewhat. In addition to revisions in the general outlook for the company noted above, other important differences between Dow's 1992 and 1997 reports can be identified. A sense of renewal and growth more effectively pervades the 1997 report, even though both reports followed years in which net income declined. The total amount of product information in the 1997 report is much larger than that in the 1992 report. The 1992 report focuses more on market conditions than the 1997 report. Dow's 1997 report provides more information that could be characterized as future-oriented. Although both reports feature an "Outlook" section for this purpose, the 1997 section is twice as long and much more specific. This may reflect a heightened corporate confidence stemming from the greater profitability reported in 1997.

5

Future-oriented/Forward-looking Information

Dow provides some future-oriented information and a few forward-looking nonfinancial performance measures. For example, statements are made with regard to the expected demand for particular products and in particular markets. There also is an occasional attempt to predict the next year's cost levels. In 1992, there is considerable effort to foretell product market entries and exits. The 1997 report incorporates a greater number of specific performance targets, as well as a higher level of future-oriented environmental discussions.

6

E.I. du Pont de Nemours and Company

Overview

E.I. du Pont de Nemours and Company (DuPont) will soon embark on its third century of continuous operations. In 1997, the firm's earnings were at record levels. The DuPont annual reports focus on reporting by segment, including transactions between segments. The reports are sophisticated, and they have numerous notable characteristics, including substantial future-oriented and forward-looking materials. Reading the 1992 and 1997 reports together provides the sense of a company transforming itself on the basis of a 10-year plan to reinvent and reinvigorate itself.

Level of Detail

Both DuPont reports are conventionally sized and 66 pages long. In this space, they provide a large amount of information. DuPont is focused on segment information. This extends, and is consistent with, DuPont's tradition of decentralized management. The five and six divisions that comprise the company in 1992 and 1997, respectively, are presented as reporting entities separately emphasized in the reports. All show financial statements with after-tax and net of extraordinary item income calculations. A large portion of the information pertains to the products that DuPont sells. As the owner of more than 2,000 trademarks and brands, the company has much to describe. Even so, the company also provides information that could be called strategic in nature, and includes details of the geographic dispersion of company operations across its major operating segments. Furthermore, financial transactions involving the company's shares (i.e., antidilutive repurchases) are well explained. Other notable transactional details include a purchased goodwill write-off treatment and sources of funding for other postemployment benefits.

Relatively Unique Content

DuPont offers several noteworthy examples of nonmandated disclosure. In its petroleum division, DuPont offers data on upstream and downstream divisions. Petroleum also offers extensive data on production and expenditure. The sales of DuPont's segments are usually disaggregated into U.S. and non-U.S. categories. DuPont provides extensive environmental disclosure. By establishing emissions goals and performance, the company provides informative content to its constituents. In addition, DuPont points out how environmental awareness has shaped new product development. Expected spending on environmental matters is detailed into compliance and remediation categories. These measures, brought to bear on the environmental issue, are unique in our sample. The company discusses a comparative treatment of effective income tax rates (EITR) in both years, explaining the cause for fluctuations. Also used is after-tax operating income (ATOI) for segments as a way of summarizing performance. The company's 1997 report gathers much of its forward-looking and future-oriented information in sections entitled "Perspective."

Structure of the Reports

Each of the DuPont reports begins with a page in which management identifies particularly newsworthy items. For example, in 1992 a 10-year strategic initiative is revealed. In 1997, a new management team reiterates its commitment to a target profit objective. Other introductory materials include tabular arrays of key performance indicators. In 1997, some of this material uses a question-and-answer format that personalizes the introduction and allows the new management to state its philosophy. The first substantive section is the CEO's letter. The letter is followed by narratives on the operating divisions. In 1992, each of the five segments has three pages of text and a one-page collage of product photos. Much of the segment review information covered in this section in 1992 is moved into MD&A in 1997, leading to more pages identified as MD&A in the latter year. The MD&A section of each report is divided into separate parts for each of the operating units. The next section is the financial statements and notes, followed by information about the board and shareholder information. In both years, supplemental sections of oil and gas segment disclosures are provided.

Orientation

The DuPont reports achieve a high sophistication level that might appeal to financial analysts and an institutional investor clientele. The use of segment performance indicators such as EITR and ATOI suggests an initiated readership that would respond to the particular fortunes and trajectories of these units. The CEO's letter is more general and appears to be written to be useful to individual investors as well as other parties.

1992/1997 Comparison

In addition to the structural similarities noted above, the DuPont reports for 1992 and 1997 have many content similarities. The aggregate amount of information in the two reports is comparable, as is the level of detail about segment operations. The 1997 report is somewhat more efficient, conveying at least the same amount of information about a more complex company in the same number of pages. The 1997 report sustains more of an integrated outlook on the future by creating a separate part of MD&A called "Perspective," which provides market outlook and discusses strategy. The 1997 report contains more information about price trends in critical markets. The heightened attention to the details on past, pending, and possible mergers; equity investments; and joint ventures in the 1997 report may reflect a substantive change in how DuPont operates as much as a change in corporate communications. The 1997 report provides a more extensive treatment of the company's environmental activities, with a longer discussion of remediation issues. The 1997 report also contains a more detailed rendering of new construction, with data on costs and expected completion dates. It can be reasonably proposed that the 1997 report is a more forward-looking review of the company. In fact, the 1997 report seems clearer on changes in the level of productive capacity throughout. Overall, however, similarities outweigh differences between the two years. This is notable given the change in top management that occurred in the interim. The style of disclosure and the segment-based reporting are important features of both reports.

Future-oriented/Forward-looking Information

DuPont's clear and unambiguous corporate performance targets are the principal elements of its future-oriented and forward-looking disclosures. For example, the company states a 15 percent target for 1992 total shareholder returns. At the segment level, the company also announces specific prioritized objectives, such as, in 1992, doubling the value of its petroleum business in 10 years and reaching the $9 billion revenue mark for fibers over four years. The emergence of the life sciences segment between 1992 and 1997 leads to the prediction that it will grow to 30 percent of DuPont's earnings in five years. The company provides insight into its capital budgeting with certain 1998 projections, including planned capital investments. Capital budgeting is framed by the phrase "think locally, resource globally," featured prominently in the 1997 report. The 1997 "Perspective" sections evaluate future demand in specific markets. Included in these sections are the company's plans to rearrange and expand productive capacity in response to these projections. The 1992 report projects the company's pollution performance for the next eight years in terms of planned reductions in pollutants and energy consumption. The 1997 report announces specific budgeted environmental spending along with a goal of zero for environmental emissions and wastes.

7

General Electric Company

Overview

The annual reports of General Electric (GE) represent sophisticated and detailed financial and nonfinancial corporate reporting. The reporting provides substantial content to readers and focuses on creating a broad appreciation for the company, its products, and its markets. The reports are also purposefully thematic, stressing "Boundaryless Behavior" in 1992 and "Six Sigma" quality programs in 1997. The latter theme is thoroughly incorporated into the fabric of the report, conveying a message that quality management is important at GE. The reports also reflect GE's decentralized operating structure. Separate divisional narratives give the reader a feel for the portfolio of operating companies that exist within the general corporate structure.

Level of Detail

GE provides specifics in virtually every sentence of every division's report, as well as in the MD&A. In both years, extensive detail is provided about the results of cost containment and quality improvement programs. Information about the development of new products is notable, not only for its frequency but also for its specificity. The tendency toward a fact-intensive orientation is ubiquitous, and is not limited to a particular division. Nor is the presentation of facts and statistics limited to the profit seeking aspects of the company. For example, in both reports GE includes a photo spread with specific examples of its community involvement through volunteers and its foundation, the GE Fund. Most of the information in the GE reports is in textual form. Pictures are used sparingly and tend to show products or employees engaged in productive processes. Pictures, in other words, are used strategically to relate factual content that might be too specific for the more generalized narrative treatment. Graphically formatted information is also limited to highly focused topics.

Relatively Unique Content

The unique contents of GE's reporting are patterned by a studied attempt to communicate the company's efforts to reengineer operations. The company has quantified these results through the many productivity gains that it reports. Some are expressed in traditional ways, with activity levels or size statistic forming the denominator. Others are freestanding monetary amounts saved as a result of implementing a particular program. Frequently, these savings are translated into their equivalent of freed factory space. This equivalence suggests a high level of sophistication regarding opportunity cost issues. The company conveys a balance between high levels of efficiency and the ability to devote resources to other purposes. GE's annual reports provide insight into the numbers that it uses to manage its enterprises, a feel for the many thresholds and stages that are involved in new product development. This is not limited to products that have government-required performance procedures, but also includes reports of products that have performed well in critical testing programs designed by the company. Both years include information on the quality of customer relationships, some of which is quantified.

Structure of the Reports

The GE reports are identical in their organization. They begin with a single page of financial highlights. GE's involvement in a large number of diverse industries would make the traditional CEO's letter rather difficult, given the company's intensive communicative intent. Therefore, the annual reports provide not only a five- to six-page letter from the CEO/chairman of the board, but also separate reports from the president of each of the dozen or so operating divisions. The CEO's letter attempts to develop explicitly the theme of the company's current initiatives. There is some attempt to mention the very highest points of operating company achievement; however, the CEO's letter tends to consider the progress and direction of the entire GE operation in a way that is different from any of the constituent companies. Thus, the CEO's letters provide the integration that would otherwise be absent. A one-page photo spread in each report amplifies the CEO's message. The divisional presidents' letters vary from one-half page to two pages, with most being one page. Their style and substance tends to be coordinated by the thematic perspective. This is obvious in 1997, as each president reports the productivity savings from Six Sigma. Otherwise, the reports are factual and similar in structure. The individual presidents' letters are followed by information about the directors and officers. The next section contains the financial statements and notes. Toward the end, an MD&A section provides more detail about each operating segment. Interspersed in the section are many short tables and bar graphs. Much additional information is provided about GE's financial transactions. Here, international operations are also dealt with in a way that cuts across operating segments. The reports conclude with one page of shareholder access information. The 1992 and 1997 reports do not differ in their structure in any material way.

Orientation

The high level of detail, the willingness to suggest strategic direction, and the systematic means of providing the bulk of the information at the operating company level of analysis suggest that GE is targeting institutional groups and sophisticated investors and analysts with its annual reports. By highlighting quality control, cross-functional teamwork, reengineering to "think small," and productivity measures, the reports target a sophisticated readership and provide little information for individual investors, even in areas where individual awareness would be high (e.g., broadcasting).

1992/1997 Comparison

Not many differences exist between the 1992 and 1997 reports. The structure and the space allotments for the reports of the divisional presidents are essentially identical. Between 1992 and 1997, GE sold its

Aerospace business, and the Motors business was combined with some other GE operations to form the Industrial Control Systems business. The most notable change over this time frame seems to be the adoption of the Six Sigma quality program, which created a theme in 1997 that was absent in 1992. Relative to the 1992 "Boundaryless" theme, the Six Sigma program appears to be more uniformly applied across operating divisions, more profound in terms of how it has changed the company, and less generic in its application. The 1997 report has also integrated more general business environment issues, most notably the Asian economic crisis and concerns over the Y2K problem. These changes probably relate more to the evolving structure of the company and its business environment than to changes in the company's communication policies. The 1997 report contains more precise information (perhaps resulting from company-wide efforts to systematize data) on productivity and quality-related savings. Nonetheless, the similarities far outweigh the differences over the two years.

Future-oriented/Forward-looking Information

GE provides considerable future-oriented and forward-looking information, including information about programs and projects that have been initiated and their future consequences. For example, expected savings from quality programs and revisions of operations are quantified and reported, usually together with results already achieved. GE also provides its expectations regarding new product performance, including what the product should be able to do, what it will replace, and when it will be ready. More specifically, GE in 1992 shares targets for order-to-delivery intervals and inventory turn reductions for particular products. Particular divisions target expected changes in revenues, especially in 1997. Suggestions for the likely composition of revenues also appear in the 1997 report. Both reports feature backlog order information that would allow a reader to project accruals.

Hershey Foods Corporation

Overview

The annual reports of the Hershey Foods Corporation give the impression of a company successfully operating behind the power of a strong market position and visible brand names. The 1992 report presents the image of a traditional, successful, small-town company. It portrays a company beginning to explore opportunities outside the United States, and one firmly grounded in employee-centered values. In 1997 the company issued a summary annual report suggesting the emergence of an increasingly professionalized management aggressively seeking to expand the company and its performance. This company appeared more able to develop the growth potential of its businesses and to make hard choices. The transition between 1992 and 1997 in the overall nature of the company is well put in a phrase used in the 1997 report: "We may look the same on the outside, but we are significantly different within." Both reports provide an appreciation for the strength of the brand names (e.g., Hershey's, Reese's) owned by Hershey Foods and the power of a company that can skillfully deploy them.

Level of Detail

The Hershey annual reports total 41 pages in 1992 and 39 pages in 1997. The 1997 Hershey Summary Annual Report does not contain the full content typically seen in annual reports (see below for more detail). Therefore, we also included a separate document entitled "1997 Consolidated Financial Statements and Management's Discussion and Analysis" in our assessment. The combination of this document with the Summary Annual Report offers information similar to that in other companies' annual reports. The reports contain detailed information such as product descriptions, market share metrics, and strategic plans.

Relatively Unique Content

Hershey provides some unique content in its reports in both qualitative and quantitative forms. In both years, Hershey offers detailed and candid views of its acquisitions and divestitures. The reports also present some of the company's strategic thinking with respect to acquisitions, the surprises that integration has produced, and other discussions of topics related to the company's experience with its acquisitions. The company reports considerable information about market share metrics, such as changes in captured market share. It breaks out sales in different points of contact with the customer (e.g., grocery store sales) for the purpose of some of these market share data. The reports describe the capital structure of Hershey Foods, giving attention to the transactions between the company and the controlling Class B shares owned by the Milton Hershey School Trust.

Structure of the Reports

The structure of Hershey Foods reports shows considerable variation over the two years, so we must treat them separately. The 1992 report follows a conventional layout strategy. A single page of graphical and tabular highlights precedes the brief but substantive president/CEO's letter, followed by a short section that praises the level of employee commitment. The most informative section in the report, entitled "Operations Review," is next. This 11-page section is organized by division, showcasing primarily the brands and products of Hershey Chocolate USA. Other divisions are geographical (Canada, International) and product-oriented (refrigerated products, pasta). Subheadings vary in these sections but tend to include new product introductions, market share growth, major marketing efforts, and capital investment. A section entitled "Financial Review" contains a seven-page MD&A that includes several bar graphs, is interspersed with financial statements, and is subdivided by general area (financial, operations, cash flows, and financial condition). Next come the notes to the financial statements. The report concludes with the auditors' letter, information about company management, and a page of investor information.

The 1997 summary annual report starts with a general introduction to the company, followed by the president/CEO's letter. The divisions are given less separate prominence in this analysis. Summary financial data come next, with no accompanying notes. Short presentations of investor information (stock price data) and management personnel follow. The supplemental 1997 document provides 11 pages of straightforward MD&A, followed by full financial statements and the associated notes.

Orientation

The fact that a summary annual report was produced in 1997 suggests that the company is orienting its annual reporting to individual shareholders. The reports establish the strong brand names that are likely to resonate with individual investors. The lack of a large body of technical information in either year suggests that the company is not focused on meeting the information needs of institutional investors or analysts. The theme of the strong market power of the company's brands might also be targeted at individual investors. Conversely, the publication of the "1997 Consolidated Financial Statements and Management's Discussion and Analysis" suggests a broader corporate communications focus that includes analysts and institutional investors. By having two documents, Hershey meets two objectives: fulfilling its technical filing requirements and offering a user-friendly glossy "advertisement" for the company that is more likely to be read by its constituents. The 1997 split between the summary annual report and a more technical document may also signal the more formal recognition of different informational needs of separate constituents.

1992/1997 Comparison

In addition to the changes in the structure of the reports, 1992 and 1997 offer two distinct reporting orientations for Hershey Foods. The 1992 report seems to portray Hershey Foods as a small-town company that is just starting to conceive of a larger agenda. This report focuses considerably on employee satisfaction and customer loyalty. The 1997 report portrays a more globally oriented, aggressively managed company. In 1992, Canada and Mexico are named as potentially important markets for the future. In 1997, a much more far-reaching exportation of business is being contemplated. The 1997 report has less division-level detail, and detailed market share information is much less common in 1997. The 1997 report also reports economic value added as a measure of corporate performance. Both reports have pictures of employees, management, products, and customers. The 1992 report features more employee pictures, and the 1997 report has more customer pictures. Whereas the 1992 report seems to cast its competitive advantage in terms of high-quality employees, the 1997 report highlights the ongoing deployment of an SAP R/3 information system as a key advantage.

Future-oriented/Forward-looking Information

The annual reports of Hershey Foods provide some general future-oriented information, including some discussion of the consequences of future raw material prices (e.g., sugar and cocoa) and the disclosure of planned capital expenditures. Both years show some future information in a variety of categories. The company is forthright about its criteria for near-term success. In 1992, it seeks to improve sales and earnings at above-market rates, to extend its consecutive annual dividend increases, and to internally finance acquisitions. In 1997, performance measurement is defined in terms of economic value added. The use of this measure establishes a basis for collection of information necessary to implement this measurement system more fully in future years.

International Business Machines Corporation

Overview

International Business Machines Corporation's (IBM's) annual reports reflect the transition of a leading company challenged by new technologies. Where the 1992 report portrays IBM as a loosely connected federation of companies, the 1997 report conveys the impression of a more focused and integrated company capitalizing on its strengths and on the interrelated needs of its customers. Both reports are designed so that the supplemental materials between the shareholder letter and MD&A convey broad messages about the industry rather than detailed information about the company, its strategies, and its operations. Both emphasize the use of graphics and images in these sections, with textual materials elsewhere in the reports. Both reports communicate company assessments of positive and negative aspects of company performance. The 1992 report, coming after a difficult year, is direct in its assessment of the company's performance. The challenges that faced the company at that time are also depicted candidly. The 1997 report, following a year of strong performance, reflects a more optimistic view of the company's future prospects. Nonetheless, the 1997 shareholder letter asserts, "... we can do better. Our consumer PC business underperformed the market in 1997." IBM represents a successful turnaround story, with its annual reports chronicling the company's course.

Level of Detail

IBM provides the greatest amount of detail about its operations, products, and markets in the MD&A section. The 1992 report disaggregates the company's operations into 15 identifiable businesses and provides broad overviews of each one's key products and performance. However, detailed product-level performance data are not typically provided. The 1997 report focuses on themes not limited to these identifiable businesses. In this year, a detailed overview of the performance of the company and its principal businesses is found in the shareholder letter. In the 1997 MD&A section, IBM provides disaggregated sales, cost of sales, and gross profit by major business. Discussions of disaggregated business sales tend to be based on full market value even though sales may have been made to other divisions at a lower transfer price. IBM's 1992 report provides greater discussion of current and planned joint ventures. The 1997 report contains more information about products, intangible assets such as patents, and attributes of the IBM workforce.

Relatively Unique Content

One of the notable features of IBM's annual reports is the use in 1997 of a four-page company timeline summarizing key events occurring during the year. IBM provides another unique "spin" in its assessment of risks and opportunities. In the 1997 shareholder letter, the company states, "... 1997 reminded us that there will always be factors beyond our control.... The final lesson of 1997 is how much of our destiny we *do* control." This candid admission is unusual in the attention that it draws to the difficulty of dealing with external events.

The 1992 report provides personnel counts for operating businesses and also discusses large work force reductions. This discussion must be understood in the context of IBM's historic reluctance to terminate employees on such a basis. The shareholder letter also mentions that a new CEO will be selected. This interjects a provisional tone to the letter. There are discussions of costs and capital expenditure reductions. Most of this is done without being very specific about the assets and the products to be affected. One financial measure noted in the 1992 report is "free cash flow."

The 1997 report has a noticeable focus on patents, devoting considerable page space to a graphical list of the many new patents awarded during the year. The report mentions the company's status as a leader in this arena several times in different places.

An interesting twist to the shareholder letter is the salutation "Dear Fellow Investor." This attempts to establish a harmony of interests by reminding readers that managers also have a considerable ownership interest.

Structure of the Reports

Both of IBM's reports begin with a shareholder letter, followed by several sections of supplemental materials. The report continues with MD&A, financial statements and notes, and other materials. The supplemental materials are different over the two reports. In the 1992 report, they are organized by major business, providing broad overviews of each business and its performance, key products, and markets. Within these sections, discussions generally highlight the more technologically advanced and most sophisticated, successful products. Another theme of this material in 1992 is the acknowledgment of poor financial performance and the steps being taken or contemplated to change this situation, including a discussion of planned cost reductions. The 1997 report, in contrast, is organized by themes that are not specifically related to the company's business. It fashions a unifying theme about things that "start here," with titles such as "The Buzz Starts Here." These sections comprise 26 pages in 1992 and 27 in 1997. In each year, a good portion is devoted to pictures (9 and 15 equivalent pages, respectively). Both reports also contain a CEO letter and an MD&A section followed by financial statements, notes, a listing of board members, and investor access information.

Orientation

The attention of the 1992 IBM report focuses on the difficult year just past and challenges ahead, and discusses IBM's strategic plans for addressing these problems. The 1997 report is far more optimistic in portraying the company as successful and favorably positioned to continue its success into the future. The supplemental sections of both reports appear geared toward a nontechnical reader. Their focus on the attempt to convey broad messages about the company's position, success, and strategic direction would seem appealing to individual investors. Technical details about the company's condition and performance are found in MD&A, to which more sophisticated investors would need to refer for more detailed and comprehensive information.

1992/1997 Comparison

The 1992 and 1997 reports find IBM in different financial positions; the company was far more successful and profitable in 1997 than in 1992. This difference is a key driver that explains the points of departure between the two annual reports. The 1997 report is more upbeat in tone, having no need to explain disappointing performance. The most notable difference in structure between 1992 and 1997 is that the 1997 report has a longer and more detailed MD&A section (10 pages versus six), and a similar difference exists in the chairman's letter. This extra length facilitates the presentation of more detailed information. For example, the 1997 MD&A presents more detailed information on major businesses, and more information about new products and financial items. These changes are only partially offset by the larger number of pictures in 1997. The 1997 report is much more specific about new product rollouts, whereas the 1992 report is more focused on discussions of prospective strategic and structural organizational changes designed to improve IBM performance. Other notable differences include the structure of the supplemental sections, organized around major businesses in 1992 and themes in 1997. Also, while free cash flow is provided in the 1992 report, by 1997 this measure is no longer included. The 1997 report contains more stock performance-oriented information. With good news to report, this information permeates the CEO's shareholder letter in 1997.

Future-oriented/Forward-looking Information

IBM explains its strategic vision, products, and market position to frame its plans for the future. Although much of the discourse in the 1992 report attempts to predict the future, few specific forward-looking forecasts are provided. Many references are made to planned cost reductions, but specific dollar goals are not disclosed. The 1992 report describes future-oriented plans for improving IBM performance in many different ways. These are generally qualitative and strategic, rather than quantitative and specific. The 1992 report mentions that the search for a new CEO would be the cornerstone of future corporate developments. The unresolved CEO succession issue may explain the absence of specific forward-looking information. Some future product development is discussed. The 1997 report presents a similar amount of forward-looking information. This information is more specific in the area of future capital investment. The 1997 report distinguishes between those aspects of the future that IBM views as within its control and outside of its control, but it does not clarify with much precision what its control will yield.

Merck & Co., Inc.

Overview

Merck is a leading pharmaceuticals company whose performance depends heavily on the development, marketing, and regulatory approval of new products. The company's annual reports reflect the importance of product development and research and development (R&D) activities in this highly innovative and comprehensively regulated environment. The reports feature discussions of Merck products, including their sales performance, fundamental characteristics and indications, R&D activities related to new products, and the company's navigation in the marketplace. There is considerable focus on strategy as the company assesses its risks and opportunities on a global basis, particularly in terms of health care regulation. Merck's reporting provides information on the science behind developing drugs and the process of bringing them to market.

Level of Detail

The Merck reports contain detailed information with respect to products and therapeutic categories. These plentiful factual data include discussions of product name; effects and uses; and potential markets for existing, new, and in-development products. Information about scientific description, intended uses, and regulatory clearance status is also presented. Revenues by product line and therapeutic category are provided. Less detail is provided about the geographic sales of product, but some analysis of international operations is included. Individual joint ventures are described. Operational and production information is less detailed, and some non-product-related aspects of the company are also not discussed with the same level of detail. Merck does provide descriptions of the workforce and characterizations of its markets.

Substantial detail is presented on marketing. Included here are Merck's strategies to partner both with other manufacturers for production and with health organizations, national pharmacies, and large employers at the consumer end. Thus, relationships with other parties are highlighted. Also in terms of relationships, the company notes its discounting of products for social welfare programs (such as vaccinations), cites its recognition as a socially conscious employer, and reviews its environmental record. In 1997, the company's exposures to currency fluctuations, inflation, and regulations are presented. For example, the prospects for the company in a managed health care environment in the United States are discussed. Nonmandated financial information includes disclosures showing how sales are affected by pricing changes. The company also discusses its pricing policy and risks, along with general, nonquantitative assessments of each product line. Detailed revenue by major therapeutic category is given, along with a presentation and discussion of costs and expenses.

Relatively Unique Content

Merck's reports contain extensive, detailed information regarding its business units. This includes a one-page summary of major units, with some operating information. A focused attempt to communicate about the people who work for Merck is conducted in both years through descriptions of the characteristics of new hires and their evaluation, training programs offered, and compensation. Merck provides a look at working relationships with other groups in the health care field (e.g., manufacturers, health maintenance organizations, and labor unions). Merck's reports provide information about product life cycles and contain background material on the illnesses or conditions a drug is intended to address. A reader could learn about the incidence of illnesses and conditions, the underlying biochemistry of the drug, and the steps in the development process for drugs. The 1997 report has a list of products organized in different ways. That year's MD&A section reports revenue by therapeutic category. The 1992 report indicates where products are in their life cycle and includes separate reports from two board committees—audit and compensation.

Structure of the Reports

The Merck reports have some structural similarities and some differences. Both start with introductory material that sets forth Merck's general growth strategy and provides current financial highlights. The 1997 report also provides an introduction to the business units that comprise the company.

The first major section in each year is the CEO's letter to shareholders. In both years, this letter focuses on the highlights of performance and profitability, new products introduced, and key research events. In addition, the fit between the environment for business and the company's strategies is articulated. Following the CEO's letter, each report has a series of topical articles, which vary in title and focus. The 1992 report begins with a treatment of major health care reform. Because this article was inspired by the governmental debate of that time, no similar material is found in 1997. The other articles in the 1992 report functionally describe the company. Sections include research, marketing, and manufacturing, along with supporting features on understanding the demand for a product, stages of product development, and partnering possibilities. These are characterized using one particular product as an example. The 1992 report also includes articles on the environment, employees, and working alliances with other companies.

The 1997 report's essays take a different approach. This report is organized by product. Articles relating to product innovation, global products, existing products, and vaccines are offered. A comprehensive list of products in reverse chronological order is also provided. Another group of essays pertains to the selling effort, with pieces on Merck's distribution and sales subsidiary, online sales efforts, and joint venture marketing. Together, the essays provide a portrait of the company, even though the organizing criteria are dissimilar.

The next substantive section is the MD&A. An extensive discussion of many matters, some of which are future-oriented, appears in that section. Financial statements and the associated notes follow. The reports conclude with information on the board and officers. The 1992 report includes short reports by the audit and compensation committees.

10

Orientation

The reports portray the company in terms of the viability of its products and its innovation. Much of the discussion of products is fairly technical; consequently, this aspect of Merck's reports seems targeted to those with health-care expertise. Other materials, such as a 10-year financial summary and the overview of principal company businesses, seem oriented toward general-purpose users. The operating detail about the company is not quantified in much detail or with much systematic organization, which suggests that the company is not oriented toward financial analysts who lack expertise in the pharmaceutical industry. The report also may be useful to readers who view new product development as a key driver of company success.

1992/1997 Comparison

The two reports are similar overall, though the information is provided in different ways. Both emphasize innovation, products, marketing the products, partnering relationships, and R&D. There is not much difference in level of detail in these areas. The 1997 report is more effective in summarizing the company's businesses. Placing an overview at the beginning of the report clarifies the structure of the company's operations. The 1992 report has more graphics on products in development. The 1992 report organizes the discussion of products by activities and markets, while the 1997 report takes a life-cycle approach to grouping products. Overall, there is more detail in the 1992 report. This may be attributed both to differences in the company at these two points in time and to differences in the format of the reports.

Future-oriented/Forward-looking Information

Forward-looking information in the Merck annual reports focuses on new product development. Discussions range from planned R&D spending to the direction of current scientific investigations to expectations about pending governmental approvals. The company also reveals plans for capital expenditures, consistent with the potential it sees in various products. The stage of development of products, together with information about where in the product life cycle existing products are, provides examples of forward-looking information in this industry. The company also discusses potential developments in the area of government regulation of health care, incidence of diseases and conditions, demographics, and general economic conditions.

PepsiCo, Inc.

Overview

In its annual reports, PepsiCo presents an array of products well known to individual consumers. Consistently, its annual reports provide a market-oriented, user-friendly perspective on corporate reporting. These reports provide a wealth of information about the history of the company's primary products. They also provide information about the competitive success of the company and, to a lesser extent, the company's plans to further that success. PepsiCo presents itself as a company well positioned to exploit the market potential of powerful beverage and food brand names.

Level of Detail

PepsiCo is a relatively focused company, and the detail given in PepsiCo's annual reports is oriented to its relative success in distinguishable geographic and product markets. Detailed market share information is provided in 1992 but not in 1997. Between 1992 and 1997, the company spun off its restaurant operations, reducing annual reporting detail. Controlling for this major restructuring, the two annual reports provide a similar depth of information. Salient levels of information are provided about the company's geographic dispersion, its merger and acquisition activity, and its efforts to alter its product offerings. The company offers a high level of information about the economic climate that it projects in the short term. The MD&A section also provides two sets of year-to-year comparisons for each of its business segments, offering a level of information that could contribute to an understanding of the company's trajectory.

11

Relatively Unique Content

Several aspects of the PepsiCo reports could be considered unique within this sample. First, the company provides detailed information about its market share in 1992. The reader learns about the competitive environment. More attention is given to descriptions of the specific product markets through recent history. PepsiCo also provides performance results denominated in poundage for its segments. On the financial side, in 1997 PepsiCo offers a specific cash flow calculation of earnings before interest, taxes, depreciation, and amortization (EBITDA), which it defines in that year's selected financial information section. Yet EBITDA does not permeate the discussion of segment results. PepsiCo provides detailed information on the performance of specific lines of business in specific countries. The company also provides a perspective on efforts to reduce costs and streamline operations toward higher levels of cost-effectiveness. Finally, it quantifies profit margins on a disaggregated basis. For example, in 1992 one can learn which menu items at Kentucky Fried Chicken generate the most income for the company.

Structure of the Reports

The structure of the PepsiCo reports is traditional. With small departures, the 1992 and the 1997 reports are similar enough to discuss together. Both reports attempt to convey a systematic theme. The 1992 report stresses the company's flexibility across the three intertwining businesses of beverages, fast-food restaurants, and packaged snack foods. In part, the flexibility pertains to running operations as diverse as beverages, foods, and fast-food restaurants. The 1997 report is entitled "Reinventing for Growth." The CEO's letter follows one page of financial highlights that feature cash flows.

The 1997 report then proceeds to an MD&A section that is subdivided into "Introduction," "Results of Operations," "Industry Segments," "Consolidated Cash Flows," and "Liquidity and Capital Resources" sections. The 1992 report offers a more complex structure involving a major (19-page, including some full-page photos) section entitled "1992 in Review." This section is subdivided into "Beverages,"

"Snack Foods," and "Restaurants." Each of these sections is then subdivided into four sections entitled "A Well-Positioned Past," "An Adaptable Present," "A Flexible Future…A Chairman's View," and "Management's Analysis." While the first two of these sections are general narratives, the third could be considered part of the CEO's letter. The fourth is explicitly cross-referenced to the subsequent two sections entitled "Management Analysis—Overview" and "Business Segments." The effort to weave across the traditional annual report sections makes it difficult to classify this portion of the 1992 PepsiCo report. Nonetheless, a large share of the annual report's information content is contained in these pages. A more traditional division is demonstrated by the 1997 report.

The next sections in both 1992 and 1997 are the financial statements and notes. In both years, additional financial data are then provided. The 1992 report contains compounded and annual growth rates for a variety of financial statement categories, 11-year comparisons, quarterly data for 1991–1992, and stock price/dividends detail. The 1997 report focuses more on segment detail. Balance sheet, income statement, and cash flow categories are subdivided into beverage and snack food segments. Additional geographic breakdowns for sales, profits, and assets are offered. Like the 1997 report, the 1992 report provides quarterly data, but its historical comparisons cover only five years of history. Both reports provide information about board members and top management, although the 1992 report is more detailed with regard to the backgrounds of the board members. It should also be noted that information (usually graphical or anecdotal) is creatively displayed in the margins of many pages, particularly in the 1992 report. Both reports make liberal use of pictures and graphical data presentation.

Orientation

The annual report of PepsiCo appears to be aimed at the individual investor. The user-friendly format and explanation of operations in simple terms seem not directed to institutional investors. Providing a more detailed historical sense is also in keeping with this focus. The strategic use of photography may create a certain level of consumer interest as well.

11

1992/1997 Comparison

It is difficult to overstate the differences between the 1992 and 1997 reports for PepsiCo. The 1992 report, at 54 pages, outstrips the 38-page 1997 report in size. Even though many more pages of the 1992 report are full-page pictures, the differences in information content appear across the board rather than being limited to a few of the categories that were used in the evaluation. Much of the difference in the reports can be attributed to the divestiture of the company's restaurant businesses. Without the need to be concerned with this market, the company reported on a reduced scope of business by 1997. The 1997 report's theme, which stresses the reinvention of the company as a more focused enterprise, provides some insight into the intensity of worldwide competition, but this perspective is rather subtle.

Future-oriented/Forward-looking Information

PepsiCo discusses strategic matters in its annual reporting. In 1997, the attention may be attributable to the need to proactively explain the recently completed spin-off of the restaurant businesses. The reports also reveal information about future capital expenditure programs. The company's likely dealings in the capital markets are also forecast. The company is willing to quantify its expected savings from restructuring efforts, particularly those projected to come from reduced labor costs.

Pharmacia & Upjohn, Inc.

Overview

Pharmacia & Upjohn (formerly Upjohn in 1992) conveys the impression of a company dedicated to advancing science, human life, and continuing corporate profitability. Its annual reports reinforce the critical value of intellectual property rights in this effort. The 1997 report conveys an increased profit-making priority with heightened emphasis on sales and achieving profit goals. The merger that produced the new company also created issues of continuity and transition that had to be addressed in the 1997 report.

Level of Detail

The two annual reports of Pharmacia & Upjohn contain 54 and 58 pages in 1992 and 1997, respectively. Overall, they provide areas of concentrated information on financing and new product development. Referred to as "new product flow" in 1997, details on current product performance and the regulatory process are provided. To accompany its extensive product data, Pharmacia & Upjohn provides equally extensive industry information. The combination would enable the reader to appreciate the company's market potential.

A third area of significant information appears in 1997 with information identifying major shareowners. In 1992, the total number of shareholders is mentioned. In 1997, the identity of the top 10 shareholders, together with their ownership amounts, is disclosed. The report further indicates steps taken to protect the existing shareholders from hostile takeover attempts.

Relatively Unique Content

Among the notable content found in the Pharmacia & Upjohn reports is coverage of the health care issue in the United States. The bearing of these developments on the company's business is especially significant. The company provides a substantial amount of product-level sales data. Both reports offer pie chart formats for geographic and product sales, revealing the company's geographical penetration and its dependence on the continuing success of particular products.

A novel measure employed in 1992 is a five-year comparison of sales per employee. In 1997, the company uses a "product freshness" index that communicates the relationship between product age and market share. In an industry driven by the episodic advance of science and the expiration of patent rights, this is a useful tool of analysis. This company also provides discussions of product pipeline issues.

Structure of the Reports

The structure of the Pharmacia & Upjohn annual reports is similar for the two years considered, even after the merger and new management. Both reports start with one page of financial highlights. In both years, graphics are employed. The CEO's letter to the shareholders is the first narrative section of both reports. Because the company's profit performance in both of the years reviewed was below expectation, both letters focus on related difficulties, and exhibit a future orientation as matters of strategy and turnaround action are discussed. A section in the 1997 letter entitled "Reshaping the Company" provides an example of this.

The next section in the 1992 report is a set of brief narratives on several of the product categories. Preceded by a short history of R&D at the company, this section informs the reader about the purpose and promise of several developmental products. In the 1997 report, this place in the report is taken by a "Strategic Overview," which discusses progress toward the achievement of five specific goals. This treatment features the combination of existing intellectual rights, scientific state-of-the-art, and government regulatory process. In 1997, a second narrative section is also included. Entitled "Company Overview," it provides the basic description of the company and its products. In both years, a tabular/graphical array of product development is introduced at this point, renamed "New Product Flow" in 1997. The major product narrative in 1997 comes at this point. This parallels the 1992 product section, except that it also includes various testimonials from patients and a more direct rendition of medical research with attestations by the scientists themselves.

A section called "Financial Review" then appears in both years. It functions as the MD&A section. Both show more details for three years of key product performance. The 1992 report features disaggregated expenses, patent expirations, and adverse publicity regarding a particular product. The 1997 report provides more information on exchange rates, sales divisions, and research and development expenditures. The two reports provide environmental information, both in terms of the company's liability for emissions and in terms of its positive remediation efforts. Pharmacia & Upjohn then presents financial statements followed by the notes and supplemental financial data, some of which are arrayed over comparative periods. The reports then present profiles of the board and top managers. Many of these people have advanced medical degrees. Shareholder access information concludes the report.

Orientation

In both years, the annual report includes content useful to analysts and institutional investors. Details on the company's product pipeline and industry data address questions that a sophisticated investor may ask. However, the report does not dwell extensively on statistical measures of performance, nor does it use proprietary calculations. The reports provide an understanding of the company that is also useful to a broader readership. In 1997, the company emphasizes its impact on quality of life. Narrative sections feature a "testimonial" story involving an individual benefiting from a Pharmacia & Upjohn product. This type of "soft" information indicates that the company uses the report to communicate with other audiences such as current and prospective employees, customers, the media, and government. Also, while the reports offer some technical medical information in the course of explaining drug development and use, they do not expect a high-level background—the information is explained in a way that can be understood by someone new to the company or industry.

1992/1997 Comparison

The 1995 merger that created the current company makes it difficult to strictly compare the 1992 and 1997 reports. Pharmacia & Upjohn represents itself as a new company in its 1997 report. Evidence of this is its changing balance between past and future orientations. Whereas the 1992 report contains more focus on past accomplishments, the 1997 report tends to spend more time looking forward to future plans.

The general difference is that the 1997 report provides more information. For example, internal technology is discussed in the 1997 report. An international patient database that provides researchers with patient management and research tools is reported on. The 1997 report is also more focused on explicit goal achievement. Here, the company announces five goals by which its performance is to be measured. The amount of industry data was increased in 1997, although it was ample in 1992.

The coverage of national and state health care reform ideas was more extensive in 1992. In 1992, the company offered 11 years of comparative information following the full financial statements, versus seven years in 1997.

The 1992 and 1997 Pharmacia & Upjohn reports also show some important similarities. Examples include the focus on pending regulatory approvals, the sales volume of specific products, and segment-level financial performance data.

Future-oriented/Forward-looking Information

A major piece of future-oriented information for Pharmacia & Upjohn is the impact of finite intellectual property protection. The financial consequences of patent expirations are related. A second area concerns pipeline management. In the 1997 report, the company indicates its goal to establish a "second pipeline" through strategic alliances with other companies. Of potential value to the uninitiated is a succinct discussion of the company's integrated product flow system.

The merger of Pharmacia and Upjohn is the base from which the future is to be projected. The effort to make the merger work addresses issues such as allocating resources and identifying a sustainable corporate culture. For the latter, the fact that the company desires "more openness to change" suggests a deepening of its future-oriented commitment.

The focus on the expected performance of future products, complemented by incremental test results information, is also consequential future-oriented information. This company is willing to share strategic information beyond its plans for specific product development. In 1997, it outlines its goals to improve sales and product mix. It also provides some clarity on anticipated expenditures. The 1992 report worked on a segment-by-segment basis in this regard, offering more general statements pertaining to the expectations for future success.

In terms of forward-looking projections, Pharmacia & Upjohn identifies "high single-digit" sales increase targets in 1997. This is complemented by the expectation of "solid double-digit growth in earnings per share." These announcements are supplemented by the company's descriptions of progress that has been made toward this goal. The reports also detail the expected effects of changes yet to be initiated.

13

Rockwell International Corporation

Overview

Rockwell projects the image of a technologically sophisticated, future-oriented firm engaged in large, multifaceted contracting activities. The wealth of details about its product development and its extensive interrelationships with public and private sector enterprises creates the impression of a strong and well-established company. Between 1992 and 1997, Rockwell restructured itself, a fact that is reflected in both the content and structure of the reports.

Level of Detail

The most concentrated area of information in the Rockwell reports centers around products. Ample treatments are given to the nature and potential of existing and future products. The company provides detailed descriptions of products under development. The report disaggregates the company into operating segments, and then discusses specific customer relationships and the performance terms in the contracts that are currently in force. In the discussion of segment performance, an assessment of performance through key operating measures, segment opportunities and risks, and brand positioning delivers a detailed treatment. Substantial attention is also given to the economic climate that currently exists and that can be anticipated. The company relies on narrative text to convey the information, with graphics and pictures used only occasionally. Rockwell also provides information about how the company's activities are allocated across its segments, explicitly presenting percentage-based descriptions.

13

Relatively Unique Content

In the 1997 report Rockwell does not include GAAP financial statements, but rather provides statements labeled as "Condensed," with a two-page summary of some information that appears to be distilled from traditional financial statement notes. This presentation is not as concise as a summary annual report, since considerable detail is provided within the other sections of the annual report. Nevertheless, it is a distinct move away from incorporating the full GAAP financial statements into the annual report.

Several other types of information are unique or notable. In 1992 the inclusion of backlogged orders, especially in tabular arrays, reflects the high proportion of the company's business with governments. Specific contract details are also found in the reports. By providing the full text of its "Credo" in both reporting years, Rockwell unifies the ideas of its mission and values. In its social reporting, the company provides information pertaining to diversity in its hiring practices and its commitment to small business in its contracting behavior. Rockwell also reveals unique measures of productivity, some based on total employees and others denominated in product volume.

Structure of the Reports

Both Rockwell reports begin with a "Financial Highlights" section that includes stock price performance. A CEO's letter to the shareholders follows. Rockwell's 1997 report includes a second letter from the retiring board chairman and a retrospective of the major corporate achievements during his tenure. The CEO's letter in both years reviews the economic climate and the overall performance of each corporate segment. The more detailed 1997 letter presents business performance in a variety of contexts, such as recent history, market competition, and comparable goals. This discussion reaches the segment and subsegment level.

In 1992, the linkage between the uncertainties of government spending and the company's prospective restructuring is described. The CEO's letters in both years also summarize the previous five years of operations in ways that extend beyond the financial statements. The

1997 letter is followed by additional financial highlights that amplify this summarization with graphics and tables.

The next portion of Rockwell's annual reports contains a series of topical narratives. Between 1992 and 1997, the specific themes varied. The 1992 report features write-ups titled "Leadership Performance," "Rockwell's Business," and "Credo." The 1997 report covers similar terrain with "Electronic Focus—Global Growth," "We Have a Track Record of Strong Performance," "We Have a Rich Heritage of Leadership in Technology and Innovation," "Rockwell Today," and "Work, Family, and Community." Thus, the 1997 report includes a higher level of precision, often breaking up the coverage of one of the 1992 sections into two sections. For example, the strategic initiatives and the use of technology reported in the 1992 report's "Leadership Performance" appear in "Electronic Focus—Global Growth" and "We Have a Rich Heritage...," respectively. Likewise, the 1992 section "Rockwell's Business" contains both performance and description of the company data. This is parsed into the "We Have a Track Record..." and the "Rockwell Today" sections of the 1997 report. The social reporting found in the 1992 report's "Corporate Citizenship" tracks into the 1997 report's "Work, Family, and Community." These sections also describe Rockwell's customer orientation and its considerable research and development commitments. Rockwell's "Credo" also appears in the 1997 report, albeit at the end of the document.

A substantive section of the 1992 annual report is the MD&A. This material appears later in the 1997 report, reversing its order with the financial data, within the context of disclosures sharing some characteristics of a summary annual report. In both years, this portion of the report covers historical trends of performance and operational matters, often on a segment-by-segment basis. A focus on R&D and capital expenditures also exists. The 1997 MD&A is more forward-oriented, with greater attention to plans and international developments, and it considers the Y2K problem. The 1997 report content also reflects the restructuring of the company.

Financial information comes next. Full financial statements and notes exist in 1992. However, summarized statements without notes are offered in 1997. Following the financial data, the reports conclude with information about the board and officers (this appears slightly earlier in the 1997 report) and general shareholder access information. The 1992 report contains a 10-year comparison of selected financial information.

Orientation

Each class of investors, current and potential, appears to be important for the Rockwell annual reports. The Rockwell reports also address the communities that the company affects. There is ample information that would be relevant to employees, not-for-profit organizations, and communities. The sizable future orientation of the Rockwell reports creates a linkage to the needs of financial analysts and institutional investors.

1992/1997 Comparison

Other than the differences pertaining to the structure of the financial data addressed above, the Rockwell annual reports' contents are quite similar. The focus on the current state of contracts with major customers and on product development is the common thread that unifies these reports.

The 1997 report provides a quantitative approach to reporting corporate performance within its narrative sections, while abbreviating the GAAP-required disclosures included in the report. Two additional narrative portions of that report are devoted to describing the trajectory of recent growth. The 1997 report also has a sharper employee focus with its consideration of the work/family balance issue. This is consistent with the broader way that Rockwell's social responsibilities are portrayed in the 1997 report. The 1997 report pays much more attention to the global nature of the company's business, and is more externally focused with more information about strategic alliances and novel partnering arrangements.

Both reports share the objective of establishing Rockwell's claim to leadership, primarily by virtue of its technological achievements. The 1997 report substantiates these claims with more information, both quantitative and qualitative. Both reports are customer-focused, although the 1997 report goes further in this regard.

Future-oriented/Forward-looking Information

One could argue that the bulk of Rockwell's reports is future-oriented, with their emphasis on the yet-to-be-completed contracts and future product development. This information is future-oriented in that it distinctly bears upon future revenues of the firm.

More specific information elements include the establishment of segment short-run goals that suggest a prioritization of the firm's attention. For example, in 1997 Rockwell announced a goal to have 40 percent of its sales sourced outside the United States. The company also projects the general economic climate that affects its businesses. This projection tends to be appropriately macroeconomic focused, given the nature of Rockwell's main businesses.

In the 1992 report, the company emphasizes its customers' expected needs as an essential part of its business, charting their ordering behavior and anticipated demand for Rockwell products. The 1997 report covers similar ground, considering partnering possibilities on a more global scale.

14

Sears, Roebuck and Co.

Overview

The annual reports of Sears portray the efforts of a large retailing company to position itself in an evolving marketplace. Its reports are focused on communicating its strategy, and as a result the 1992 and 1997 reports are very different. In 1992, the major objective was to give the reader a feel for the diversity of enterprises the company managed. The 1997 report shows a different company that wants to use the annual report to continue to tell about its ongoing efforts to reinvent itself through corporate restructuring. The 1997 report pertains to a more focused, more unified company, relating its culture, its customer orientation, and its linkages to the broader community. Despite the fact that the 1997 report also had to deal with financial reverses, it does so on a much different basis. It provides specific strategies for improved performance, grounded in its new thinking about customers and employees.

Level of Detail

Sears provides both quantitative and qualitative detail. The detail found in the 1992 and 1997 reports is considerably different, however. In 1992, performance statistics on the major business sectors are comprehensively reported. Sears takes this approach one step further by breaking out major subsegments for a similar detailed analysis. Segments and subsegments are then placed in a historical context through the reporting of previous performance levels. The divestitures that occurred between 1992 and 1997 made this approach no longer viable. The 1997 report compresses the segmental reporting that remains in favor of a more precise description of retail properties and product composition. The 1997 report also provides a higher level of detail about marketing efforts and the specific profitability and growth of certain customer offerings. Both reports provide ample detail about the company's history and its continuing charitable activities. Both reports present a strategic agenda.

Relatively Unique Content

Sears offers some unique content in both of its annual reports. The disaggregation of financial information in the 1992 report is done with stand-alone financial statements, each with its own notes, for the major sectors. Sears also provides multiple perspectives on its businesses by offering other disaggregated information, including specific performance indicators. Along these lines, pro forma statements are offered that distinguish operating results inclusive and exclusive of discontinued operations. The totality of these efforts should be considered a unique approach to reporting in this sample.

In 1992, Sears also provides nonmandated statistics on employees and suppliers, focusing on their ethnic, gender, and racial diversity. The notable content in the 1997 Sears report pertains more to the details of running a multiproduct merchandising operation. This entails more information on the number and location of its stores, its deployment of advanced technologies to enhance customer service, and the specifics of its marketing campaigns. The 1997 report provides more qualitative detail on relationships with external parties (e.g., customers and suppliers). Sears in 1997 provides historical data on its market capitalization and presents its key financial ratios.

Structure of the Reports

The 1992 and 1997 Sears reports are substantially different in their structure. The 1992 report provides traditional content in a disaggregated way. It begins with an overview of Sears, including a graphical representation of its segments, separated into "core," "ongoing," and "other" operating units, followed by a table of three years of financial highlights. The third section is a three-page "Chairman's Message to Shareholders," which contains an overall evaluation of the company and its operating unit performance, as well as strategies for improved performance and expectations for future economic conditions. The fourth section lists directors and officers, including board committee memberships. The next section, "Financial Services Group Analysis," describes an alternatively defined segment that groups together all the Sears service segments and discusses strategy, competitive position, and historical performance of the operating units comprising this segment. The section entitled "Financial Objectives" assesses the company's financial performance, including cost-of-capital measures, shareholder returns, company strategic planning, and restructuring, by refocusing on "core" operations, and assesses future prospects for the company's core businesses.

The next five sections assess major operating segments of Sears: Sears Merchandise Group, Allstate Insurance Group, Dean Witter, Discover, and Coldwell Banker. The level of detail varies over these units, with far more discussion devoted to Sears Merchandise and Allstate. The Sears Merchandise section includes descriptions of its competitive position and comparative advantages, customers, marketing focus and plans by product line, a discussion of products and product brands, expansion plans, and new customer service initiatives. Allstate begins with a discussion of major catastrophes affecting this group, then disaggregates its analysis into its three different insurance subsegments. Discussions include revenue measures, competitive position, strategies, use of information technologies, and the performance of further disaggregated segments.

The next section contains a 10-year summary of key financial statistics, followed by a 5-year summary of revenues, net income, and assets by business group. Then the company's consolidated financial statements and accompanying MD&A are presented. MD&A includes discussions of strategic repositioning, analysis of operations, debt ratings, a graph of segment assets, a historical graph of funding sources, unaudited quarterly results, and stock market information.

Next, the Sears Merchandise Group summary financial statements and analysis are presented. The analysis includes discussions of operations, restructuring, and further disaggregations into the subsegments of merchandising, credit operations, and international operations. For each subsegment, selected financial performance and condition numbers are provided, accompanied by selected pertinent ratios. Similarly, financial statements for Allstate are presented. Finally, a section on

"Corporate Responsibility" discusses the company's activities in the areas of charitable contributions, sponsorship of educational programs, community involvement, employment diversity statistics, and statistics on the purchases of goods and services from minority-owned firms.

The 1997 report favors a magazine-style presentation, complete with advertising and coupons and introduced by a magazine-style table of contents. A large portion of the report consists of essays that relate to the strengths of Sears. Following a table that provides three years of financial highlights, the chairman's letter gives an overall company and business-based analysis of performance, then discusses customer satisfaction, company market value, future prospects, and strategic focus—overall and in some specific businesses.

In the next section, entitled "What It Takes to Win," the company presents its strategies in more detail, including managerial ethics, employee compensation, and community activities, as well as a focus on employee attitudes, customer satisfaction, and financial performance. The following section, "Strong Enduring Customer Relationships," addresses customer relationships and highlights the use of information technology in improving both customer service and marketing. Specific marketing programs are discussed.

A subsequent article, "Expanding Network of Store and Home Services," discusses the company's strategy and mission; its segments and their respective strategies; and markets, brands, products, and plans for expansion and growth. An insert entitled "Sears, Roebuck and Company" concisely describes company segments and subsegments. "Marketing and Merchandising Expertise" focuses on company marketing and sponsorship strategies and programs. This section includes specific examples and highlights the use of new marketing media (e.g., the Internet). "Broad Range of Proprietary and National Brands" describes the products Sears offers. In addition to descriptions of both new and existing products, the strength of associated brand names, and the value of proprietary and exclusive interests, this section discusses company objectives regarding product quality. Selected statistics on sales of some products are also presented in this section. "Community Service" describes the company's activities in terms of volunteer hours, charitable contributions, community involvement, program sponsorship, and recycling. When this is followed by the company's 1997 financial statements, the annual report reverts to a more conventional format. Although the formal statements are consolidated, results and analysis by segment and subsegment are presented in the subsequent discussion, which includes supplemental information, such as an earnings forecast, an analysis of international operations, debt ratings, description of capital spending, and selected ratios and statistics. Following the financial statements are a five-year selected financial summary, quarterly results, common stock information and dividends, an analysis of market risk related to financial information, a description of executive officers, and a list of board members and their committee memberships.

Orientation

In both years, Sears' annual reports appear to include the level of information that institutional shareholders and analysts would find desirable. Along these lines, segment details and a significant array of size, production, expansion/consolidation, and strategy facts are forthcoming. To a lesser extent, the report could be understood by a new individual investor as well, since the corporate overview snapshots and product descriptions introduce newcomers to the company in a way consistent with their experience of Sears as consumers. In 1997, Sears' reporting seems to be more balanced between individual shareholder and institutional analyst. The individual investor may be the more apt target audience for the messages about corporate culture and values. The magazine format should also appeal to that group. In 1997, the Sears report appears to be designed (photos, ads, coupons) to persuade the reader to also become a customer—an effort that did not appear to be undertaken in 1992. For the sophisticated investor there is still a substantial amount of operational detail, and an increased focus on the company's strategies (use of information technologies in marketing, customer relations, and inventory management) and comparative advantages (such as brand names, customer satisfaction, and competitive position).

1992/1997 Comparison

Sears was a fundamentally different company in 1992 and in 1997, and as a result, reporting differences are to be expected. Many of these have been noted above. Therefore, only the similarities bear further elaboration. Sears, in both years, seems committed to informative reporting, which entails providing precise information about operations that goes beyond what is statutorily required. Sears also demonstrates a customer orientation in both reports. This orientation appears more obvious in 1997, after the company had focused on fewer different activities. A strong marketing orientation also appears in the annual reports. Again, 1997 provides a more explicit example.

Future-oriented/Forward-looking Information

As to forward-looking predictions, Sears attempts to use the annual report to establish target profitability measures for the short term. These include, in 1992, target return on assets and two-year return on equity and, in 1997, a prediction of expected segment earnings (on a selected basis). In 1997, overall earnings are forecast to be modestly up after expected declines in the first quarter. In nonfinancial matters, Sears provides some future-oriented information, for example in the 1992 report, projecting the number of employees who would be eliminated following restructuring. In the 1997 report, Sears predicts the total number of stores that will be operating in 2000.

15

Wal-Mart Stores, Inc.

Overview

Wal-Mart's annual reports emphasize various nontraditional information content items of corporate annual reporting. In addition to profitability and cash flow metrics, Wal-Mart emphasizes the physical and geographical growth of its operations. Facility location and the cumulative number of locations are important elements of these reports. Other size statistics are also mentioned. Wal-Mart focuses on the personal details of employees' and board members' lives. The company also provides great detail about its community involvement and charitable activities. In addition to highlighting these nontraditional content areas, Wal-Mart communicates with nontraditional methods. Its use of maps gives the reader a feel for the geographical dispersion of the company. In 1997, Wal-Mart adopted a magazine format that explored novel ways of talking about the company. Consistent with this format, some pages are devoted entirely to "ads" for the company's exclusively marketed products.

Level of Detail

Partly reflective of its emphasis on the subjective aspects of its business (i.e., family attitude toward employees, value orientation for its customers), the bulk of Wal-Mart's commentary is different from a traditional approach. Wal Mart's 1992 annual report is 22 pages, while its 1997 annual report is 38 pages. The company emphasizes extensive detail pertaining to the size and location of its stores, and gives detail about its information technology, its employees, and its strategic plans to focus on new markets and new ways of attracting customers.

15

Relatively Unique Content

The unique content in these reports occurs, for the most part, in the areas on which the company has chosen to focus. The size statistics mentioned above are not only reported for the company as a whole but are also a means of charting the relative progress of the company's three types of facilities (stores, clubs, and superstores). A growth objective is manifested in this way as the company employs as a metric the amount of same-store sales. The company provides average volume of sales activity by type of store. Successful past growth is highlighted through 10-year summary financial and nonfinancial statistics. To demonstrate the international appeal of its customer offerings, special emphasis is placed on stores located outside the United States. Anecdotal treatments of store openings and store offerings in nations such as Mexico and China are featured. The company reports the extent of customer traffic in some of its new stores abroad, and in the 1997 report provides information about its efforts to employ inventory technology. Wal-Mart provides many facts about its charitable activities, giving specific dollar amounts, especially in 1997. It offers detailed profiles of board members and employees, providing information about their lives beyond their relationship to the company (e.g., admirable qualities, hobbies, personal background).

Structure of the Reports

The differences in the 1992 and 1997 Wal-Mart annual reports preclude any attempt to develop a common structure. For 1992, the year in which founder Sam Walton died, the report follows a fairly conventional organization. Two introductory pages (including a tribute to the late founder) precede a two-page president's letter (titled "Dear Partner"). This section implies a commonality of interests between the company and its constituents. The president's letter is divided into financial, operational, and strategic sections. A two-page map of the United States appears at this point. A count of store locations by state is provided as an index to this map. Then, a 10-year financial summary is placed as a prelude to the two-page MD&A. The full financial statements and the associated notes are then presented. The report concludes with the audit opinion and two pages of board and officer names. Key addresses are provided here as well.

The 1997 report follows a popular magazine format. In addition to having a very nontraditional annual report cover, it is organized with a stylized set of magazine features, such as a magazine-style table of contents, full-page "ads" highlighting product joint ventures, and a high picture-to-text ratio. A two-page president's letter is the first substantive section. Unlike 1992, the 1997 president's letter is not analytically divided and is much less formal in its orientation. The letter is followed by detailed profiles (and pictures) of the Wal-Mart board. The next five sections present pictures and stories about the company's community involvement and history.

The first of the "magazine's" main articles describes how the opening of a Wal-Mart store improved life in a specific community. The second article describes Wal-Mart's contribution to a charitable organization, the Children's Miracle Network. The next describes the role of technology in improving Wal-Mart's inventory management. Another describes Wal-Mart's increasing presence outside the United States. Throughout these articles are ads for new Wal-Mart products (e.g., credit cards, exclusive merchandise).

Other articles spotlight particular Wal-Mart employees. The next two stories describe the company's efforts to build superstores and to sell memberships. The report returns to a more conventional format toward its end, with business information placed in geographic context. At this point, financial summaries are provided that would allow the reader to compare the current year with the previous 10 years. This array of financial information is followed by a brief MD&A and financial statements and notes. The report concludes with more full-page pictures, the auditor's report, and a page of information for shareholders.

Orientation

The 1992 Wal-Mart report appears to be oriented toward individual investors. Its focus on the growth of stores across the United States makes a strong appeal in this direction. There does not appear to be any particular informational content that would suggest an orientation toward financial analysts. The 1997 report, with its unconventional magazine style, also tips toward those investors who would enjoy the unusual, folksy portrayal. The 1997 report has a strong orientation toward constituents other than investors. Its focus on community involvement and its positive impact on local economies sends a strong message to state and local policy makers.

1992/1997 Comparison

The 1992 report provides an overview of Wal-Mart that might be of interest to anyone wishing to obtain a basic understanding of the company, without a focus on any particular constituencies (shareholders, creditors, employees, customers, or communities). In contrast, the 1997 report appears to be oriented more toward the general public than toward any specific constituent group. The company does not dwell on the traditional profitability metrics that would be the primary focus of institutional or individual investors. The extent of profit growth and share price increases is reported but is not given great prominence. Wal-Mart addresses the issue of corporate citizenship directly. The notion that Wal-Mart can be a prominent positive force in a community by providing employment and community commercial revitalization is extensively detailed.

The 1992 and 1997 reports have similarities and differences beyond the structural departures noted above. The 1997 report focuses on communicating corporate values, mission, and culture. The 1992 report provides information about the direction and magnitude of company expansion. The 1992 report also provides more investor-relevant information. The 1997 report is focused on marketing company products. Neither report provides in-depth information about specific product lines or marketing strategy. The 1992 report contains less discretionary material (4 pages compared with 21 for 1997). The 1997 report provides more information that would be relevant to groups other than shareholders. By adopting a magazine format, the 1997 report makes interesting reading for community decision makers, customers, and employees as well as shareholders and analysts. The 1997 report is clearer about the company's relationships with other corporations, particularly joint merchandising efforts.

Future-oriented/Forward-looking Information

The future orientation of Wal-Mart is indicated by the specific mention of future planning in both the 1992 president's letter and MD&A. The concentration of specific future-oriented nonfinancial information in the 1992 and 1997 reports occurs around the issue of future store locations and the money that will be invested toward that purpose. Wal-Mart projects its cash-generating ability to finance growth in 1997. It also signals which store types it has designated a priority. Within its superstores, Wal-Mart reports also indicate a direction of some particular departments (e.g., enhancing grocery departments). Some forward-looking predictions are provided as both reports touch lightly on future performance targets. A targeted shareholder rate of return is identified in 1997. Sales predictions are briefly mentioned in 1992. That report also qualitatively ties improved sales and market share to enhanced service (wider aisles, faster checkout). This may indicate future strategy. The company shows how past predictions (from 1990) have been exceeded, but it does not, in the 1997 report, provide new predictions.

16

Westvaco Corporation

Overview

Westvaco, a manufacturer of paper products for a variety of uses, issues annual reports that follow a traditional format that serves to provide a basic understanding of the company and its products. It does not sell distinctive brands to the mass market. The 1997 report, focusing on globalization, offers an enhanced focus. The 1992 report contains a retirement tribute that identifies the Luke family lineage, shared by a former CEO, a former director, the current chairman of the board, the current CEO, and the town of primary operations.

Level of Detail

Westvaco provides some nonmandated, nonfinancial information, including considerable detail about the company's products and its operating divisions. Items pertaining to the operating capacity of various company facilities are supplied. The company details more than the required information about employee compensation. A lesser amount of detail pertains to corporate structure, marketing, and strategy. The information in the reports appears across sections. Throughout these reports, information tends to be descriptive and qualitative, rather than analytical and quantitative. For example, the company often describes itself as a leading producer of a certain product but does not provide its market share or the amount it produces relative to its competitors. Almost all the information appears in textual form; few graphs and charts are employed. Pictures are also used sparingly and, when used, depict products or employees.

16

Relatively Unique Content

Market price for Westvaco's products is a key factor for its success. Therefore, Westvaco provides considerable detail about changes in the prices its products command. There also is a high level of detail about environmental performance, in both a compliance and a forestry R&D sense. As a paper products company, Westvaco seeks to convey to the reader that it is an environmentally friendly company seeking to discover additional products. There is also added information about employees (e.g., distribution, compensation, and attributes). The company provides micro-level detail about specific new products and particular capital projects. The performance of new products also is described. The expected productive capabilities of new facilities are detailed. Traditional financial ratios used to measure profitability, liquidity, and solvency are explicitly presented.

Structure of the Reports

The 1992 and 1997 reports are similar in structure. Three pages of introductory matter include information for shareholders (e.g., annual meeting location, dividend payments, access detail), an introduction to the report's theme, and financial data highlights. Both themes involve the idea of focus and the process of continuous innovation. The 1992 report adds shareholder value, while the additional parts of the 1997 theme are global vision and customers. A CEO's letter follows, discussing the fit between the economic outlook and the company's products, both in terms of the past year and the near future. Each letter has a mix of descriptions of the firm's principal products and their fit within the evolving marketplace.

The next section of each report is a set of thematic essays that provide a slightly more detailed review of the year's operations. The 1992 report provides treatments entitled "Our Sound Business Strategy," "Westvaco's Team Spirit," and "Environmental Stewardship." In 1997, the areas are titled "Strategy," "Strength," "Value," and "Rewards." However, two of the 1997 topics are single pages dominated by photography, so the report does not add new content areas. A focus on company strategy is a characteristic of this area of the report. In 1992, a special section draws particular attention to the company's environmental practices. There is no equivalent section in 1997, although environmental issues are noted in the CEO's letter and in the MD&A.

Both reports then provide the content typically found in MD&A, although it is labeled "Financial Review." The section is three partial pages in 1992 and four full pages in 1997, subdivided into major sections called "Liquidity and Capital Resources," "Analysis of Operations," and shorter treatments of dividend reinvestment plans, number of shareholders, and payroll and benefit costs. In addition, the MD&A section puts the company's current year in context with short narrative summaries of the previous two years.

In 1997, the major MD&A sections are internally subdivided into the company's three major operating segments (bleached, unbleached, and chemicals). The financial statements (in both years preceded by a concise financial summary focusing on the previous three years) follow. The sections give a capsule narrative on sales, income, profit margins, costs, and major changes in productive facilities. However, no explicit comparisons between years are made. The notes reveal four business segments defined by product type (bleached, unbleached, chemicals, and corporate items). These segments are not employed elsewhere as an organizing theme in the reports. Both reports contain an 11-year financial summary following the financial statement notes. Completing the report is more information about the company's personnel and its locations. The location information includes a list of the cities where production facilities and sales offices can be found.

Orientation

The shareholder-returns information in the Westvaco reports suggests that the reports are oriented to a general audience of individual investors. Conversations appear to be aimed at existing shareholders, with the message that management is persevering in a difficult economic and competitive environment. There is balance in the reports with some orientation toward employees and toward a larger community (e.g., environmentalists, government regulators).

16

1992/1997 Comparison

The 1992 and 1997 reports are identical in structure. The continuity of the CEO, in his first (1992) and sixth (1997) years, respectively, explains this consistency of focus. A continuity of business operations may also contribute to the continuity of style in these annual reports. However, a higher level of detail was noted in the 1997 report. Specifically, the 1997 report improves upon descriptions of the firm's properties, capacities, new product plans, and relationships with particular customers. It also contains more commentary about the economic health of Westvaco's product markets, and it has more visual materials than the 1992 report. Since Westvaco provides packaging for a variety of products, pictures communicate the depth and variety of Westvaco's customer base.

In addition to product pictures, the 1997 report employs photographs of its production facilities, while the 1992 report has more photos of employees. Part of the increased information in 1997 may be a result of the international growth of the company during the intervening years. This international growth is addressed in the first part of Westvaco's 1997 theme, "Global Vision, Customer Focus, Innovation." The 1997 report also identifies product niches that appear more secure and better defined. This development is reflected in a shift of information from MD&A to that included in other narrative sections of the report. The 1997 report addresses Westvaco's focus on external standards (e.g., ISO 9000) and business environment problems (e.g., Y2K, the Asian economic crisis).

Future-oriented/Forward-looking Information

The company presents future-oriented information more than forward-looking predictions. The company provides some directional indications of its intentions to move toward product sectors and geographic areas with greater potential. It also discusses levels of expected capital expenditures with specifics on selected projects to be completed in the short term. Projected future borrowing is also discussed. By far the most frequently mentioned future-oriented issue is the expected movement of prices; the company's dependency on general price movements is made clear in both reports.

APPENDIX A

Literature Review

There have been a number of studies on the value of company annual reports and other corporate communications with investors during the past two decades. Although perennially a topic of interest to the business community, financial reporting has received increased attention since the publication of the American Institute of Certified Public Accountants' (AICPA) *The Information Needs of Investors and Creditors*, the "Jenkins Committee Report" (AICPA, 1993), which recommended a "business reporting" model incorporating disclosures in a number of key areas. Following this work, the Financial Accounting Standards Board (FASB) has undertaken study of certain aspects of existing corporate communications from the Business Reporting Model perspective. For the financial preparer community, corporate communications (including financial reporting) are of interest for several reasons. On one hand, preparers are interested in understanding how corporate communications and financial reporting can create value for the company, its investors, and other interested parties. On the other hand, preparers are concerned about possible financial reporting regulation that imposes additional costs on companies without creating value for the company or its stakeholders.

While annual reports have a long history, it was not until the 1930s that U.S. securities legislation established disclosure requirements for publicly traded firms. Requirements have evolved over time, and include annual reporting of financial and nonfinancial information in financial reports. Annual reports now contain several key elements, including a set of financial statements with related notes and auditor's opinion, a CEO's letter, and MD&A. Regulations have also specified that certain types of disclosures and discussions be included in a company's financial report. These requirements leave considerable latitude in constructing annual reports, such that companies can provide substantially more information than required, either within the disclosure elements listed above or in other supplemental sections.

APPENDIX A

There is growing recognition by companies of the potential value of engaging in an active communication process with the investment community and other interested parties. Some studies have suggested real economic value, in terms of company cost-of-capital and other measures, to disclosing information about the company beyond that required. Chief financial officers of large companies have called corporate communications with the investing community one of the most important activities of their organizations (Rivel Research Group, 1996).

From the broad corporate communications perspective, a company's annual report is an important, but usually not exclusive, component of its communication program. Corporate communication could also include things such as fact books or fact sheets, news releases, Web sites, and meetings or conference calls with analysts or investors. New communication and information technologies have simultaneously increased the types of media and decreased the cost of communicating directly with all elements of the investment community and other interested parties. Consequently, companies' choices of communications with the investment community involve not only matters of disclosure content but also delivery media. Nonetheless, the annual report remains a centerpiece of corporate communication. Its historical and symbolic value are unrivaled, even though other means of conveying information exist. The breadth of its distribution also makes it uniquely able to convey the company's message.

The Use and Value of Annual Reports

Despite the apparent increased interest of companies in corporate communications, there is a long history of concern about the adequacy of accounting reports in meeting the information needs of investors and other interested parties. Illustrative is Rimerman's 1990 *Journal of Accountancy* article, "The Changing Significance of Financial Statements," in which the author emphasizes "the fundamental change in the general business environment in which users' needs have grown beyond GAAP financial statements." Concern has also been expressed about the informativeness of nonfinancial disclosures in annual reports (Mahoney, January 1999, February 1999), as well as the quality of disclosures (Levitt, 1998). A Shelley Taylor and Associates Survey

(Mahoney, January 1999) concludes that required disclosures meet only a portion of institutional investors' needs. Taylor asserts that "voluntary disclosure plays a pivotal role in providing investors with the operational and financial information they require to make sound investment decisions" (p. 15).

A number of studies have addressed the value of annual reports to investors and other parties. One approach has been to survey analysts and other sophisticated users of financial information, often asking them to rate or rank the importance or adequacy of particular kinds of information. Lee and Tweedie (1977, 1981, 1990), for example, conducted detailed interviews of investment professionals on this issue. A study sponsored by the Financial Executives Research Foundation (FERF) (SRI International, 1987) surveyed analysts on the frequencies of use of information sources, importance of information sources, and types of information of interest. It reported that the most-used source of information was the company annual report. Within the annual reports, the five types of information of most interest to surveyed analysts were recent developments and outlook for the company's industry, annual company earnings, company's position in the marketplace, risks to the company, and recent significant events.

This FERF study summarized analysts' opinions that financial reports could be improved by providing more information on the company's market and competitive position, business segment financial statements, intra-industry comparisons, management goals and objectives, and company performance statistics and ratios. Thus, from the perspective of knowledgeable users, the information content of annual reports can clearly be improved. Other studies, not limited to the interests of a single user group, reach similar conclusions. For example, Hill and Knowlton (1984) reported that financial reports were ranked second in importance only to direct discussions with management.

The Special Committee on Financial Reporting, formed by AICPA in 1991 to study business reporting relevance and usefulness, offered the Business Reporting Model. The research and study leading to the development of this model was conducted by the committee and academicians, such as Previts et al. (1993). This model recommended that companies communicate "high-level operating data and performance measurements that management uses to manage the business," "more forward-looking information," "opportunities and risks," "management's plans and strategies," and "comparisons of actual business performance to...plans," in addition to traditional disclosures. The report's recommendations led to discussions of the merits of the Business Reporting Model, such as "FEI Challenges Preliminary Findings of AICPA Special Committee" (FEI, 1993). The Special Committee's final report was published in 1993 (AICPA, 1993). Around the same time, the Association for Investment Management and Research (AIMR) published Knutson's study *Financial Reporting in the 1990's and Beyond* (1992), which examined financial analysis processes and the views of financial analysts on financial reporting. This position paper also recommended certain financial reporting changes.

This line of study attracted the attention of the FASB, which in 1996 issued an "Invitation to Comment" on both the Jenkins Committee and AIMR Report recommendations. The first question posed by the invitation was "Should the FASB broaden its activities beyond financial statements and related disclosures to also address the types of nonfinancial information that would be included in a comprehensive business reporting model?" Responses to the FASB's invitation were mixed. In early 1998, the FASB decided to move forward on a business-reporting project. While there has been concern that the FASB's project is an exercise that could lead to additional standard setting, its letter inviting companies to participate in the project suggests a benchmarking objective. According to the letter, "The ultimate goal of the research project is to call attention to highly effective disclosures that some companies are now voluntarily furnishing, so that others might follow their lead" (FASB, 1998). This view is consistent with a 1995 survey of corporate managers, financial analysts, and portfolio managers that found little support for the increased regulation of financial reporting (Eccles and Mavrinac, 1995). That study recommended improved voluntary reporting of nonfinancial information.

The AICPA and AIMR studies also led to studies in the academic community on the value of nonfinancial information. This group of studies examined the types of information used by financial analysts in the production of their reports. Included in these data is nonfinancial information such as market share, competitive position, industry and economic conditions, competitors' capabilities, and products. Previts et al. (1994) found that analysts actively seek such types of information. Similarly, Rogers and Grant (1997) show that a high proportion of information actually used by analysts in the production of their reports can be found in company annual report narratives. In another recent survey, Epstein and Palepu's (1999) survey of 140 "star" analysts found that they regard annual reports as important, particularly MD&A and the president's letter. Regarded as not important were a company's balance sheet and the essay and pictorial section. The most valuable types of information were segment performance data and the financial statements. They assert, "By making financial reports more central to a communications strategy, companies can improve relations with stakeholders and analysts." They also note how corporate communications can improve management credibility.

The idea of company communications as a strategic voluntary, rather than regulatory, activity has also been recognized by leading business service firms. PricewaterhouseCoopers, for example, has published a series of papers on voluntary company communications. Their survey of professional investors and analysts reflects, in part, respondents' beliefs about the value of improved corporate disclosure, led by increased management credibility, increased number of long-term investors, and increased share value.

The sixth paper in the PricewaterhouseCoopers series, *Pursuing Value: The Information Reporting Gap in the U.S. Capital Markets* (Eccles and Kahn, 1998) assesses, in part, the usefulness of company disclosure to investors and analysts. Virtually all investors and analysts surveyed agree that companies provide "additional information" that they consider "useful." Forty to 50 percent of those surveyed responded that companies provide additional information except when such information might be sensitive or proprietary. The survey found that the most important performance measures (average of investor and analyst responses) were cash flows, R&D, earnings, market share, capital expenditures, new product development, costs, market growth, employee productivity, segment performance, and statements of strategic goals. Four "unimportant measures," according to the survey results, were employee training, process quality, employee turnover, and employee satisfaction. Over 60 percent of respondents reported that companies were doing an "adequate" job of reporting in the areas of cash flows, R&D, earnings, market share, capital expenditures, market growth, and statements of strategic goals.

This body of research suggests that annual reports are valuable to investors because they contain supplemental information that is relevant to forecasting the future performance of a firm. At the same time, they suggest that there are many areas for continued improvements. The Epstein and Palepu (1999) survey, for example, reported analyst desire for "more information on business risks and uncertainties, financial liquidity and flexibility...(and) strategy." Analysts asserted that annual reports infrequently provide adequate information about a company's risks and uncertainties. Other frequently cited requests included product line and segment performance data and a budgeted income statement in MD&A.

The Use and Value of Particular Disclosures

Some studies have sought to identify with greater precision the value of particular disclosures. Items that have been considered include forward-looking information, alternative performance measures, capital expenditures, MD&A, segment disclosure, management quality, intangibles, and company competitive position.

Recent safe harbor legislation has reduced company legal exposure in making certain forward-looking statements, broadening the opportunities for corporate communications within the annual report. Previts et al. (1994), and Bricker et al. (1995) noted that analysts consider information that is predictive of future earnings to be of great value. However, such disclosures may not always be specific or quantified forecasts. That is, company annual reports may contain both "forward-looking" and "future-oriented" content. Forward-looking content refers to specific forecasts and estimates of future performance that are covered under the safe harbor rules. Mahoney (May 1999) notes that "companies are still in limbo, since court tests still haven't gone through definitive appeals process, and given us precedent to work from." Mahoney also cites other expert opinions that companies use too much boilerplate safe harbor language and fail to link safe harbor disclaimers to specific forward-looking statements. In contrast, some content may have a future orientation without containing specific forecasts or estimates of future performance. Such future-oriented content might include the company's strategic plan, information about its plans for expansion or downsizing, new products, and a general assessment of company risks and opportunities (Previts et al. 1993).

Johnson et al. (1998) suggest that companies in the high-technology field have responded to the new safe harbor provisions both by more frequently including forecasts and by making forecasts more precise. The SEC has signaled its interest in encouraging (or requiring) certain forward-looking information in a recent release. The SEC specifically wants public companies to describe company risk factors—things that "may have a negative impact on the [company's] future financial performance" (Yurow, 1999). Furthermore, the SEC wants discussions of risk to be more clearly and plainly worded.

Some studies addressed possible value drivers as alternative performance measures. Previts et al. (1993) note that both general information about future products, projects, and restructurings and specific information about orders, backorders, and shipments are consequential in analysts' attempts to predict future earnings. Peterson (1998) wrote, "Many companies have embraced—and many others felt obligated to look at—performance measures that depart from traditional accounting-based measures such as earnings per share and return on investment" (p. 15). These new value-based measures include economic value added, market value added (MVA), and refined economic value added (REVA). Amir and Lev (1996) demonstrated the value relevance of such industry-specific nonfinancial indicators in the wireless communications industry. They defined nonfinancial measures as quantitative measures of performance not contained in traditional financial statements.

Kerstein and Kim (1995) found a strong association between the disclosure of capital expenditures and above-market stock returns. Both Bryan (1997) and Barron et al. (1998) found share value associated with disclosure of planned capital expenditures. Previts et al. (1993, 1994) also noted analyst attention to capital expenditures.

Several studies have suggested the importance of MD&A to investors. Rogers and Grant (1997) showed that much of the content of analyst reports can be linked to company narratives such as MD&A. Similarly, Bryan (1997) analyzed seven required MD&A disclosures and found them to be associated with near-term performance. Barron et al. (1998) surveyed a number of studies of MD&A and concluded that it is of value to analysts because it is likely to contain information on forward-looking trends and infrequent events.

Another theme is segment disclosure. The Hill and Knowlton (1984) study recommended a high level of detail about the business that can be approached on a segment-by-segment basis. A comprehensive study of segment reporting sponsored by the Canadian Institute of Chartered Accountants found that sell-side analysts appeared to rely more heavily on segment details (Boersema and Van Weelden, 1992). Similarly, Previts et al. (1993, 1994) found that analysts typically disaggregate company performance beyond the segments reported by the company. These results confirm the findings of the SRI International (1987) survey that shows investor preferences for more detailed segment reporting.

Intangibles have also become an issue to investors. The value of brand names, research and development expenditures, and other intellectual property is difficult to measure with traditional financial statements. While Previts et al. (1993, 1994) found that analysts tend to assess companies on the basis of asset costs, exceptions were noted for companies with significant off-balance-sheet assets. Several firms are currently working on approaches to better valuing and communicating the values of intangible assets (Mahoney, April 1999).

Executives and investors share the opinion that analysts often do not fully understand the company and its principal strategies, although 68 percent of analysts disagree with this assessment (Eccles and Kahn, 1998). These results are echoed by Epstein and Palepu (1999), who assert that "senior corporate executives commonly believe that capital markets do not properly understand and value their strategies and that financial analysts as information intermediaries are primarily to blame." While a recent Shelley Taylor and Associates Survey report confirmed that this is among the most important subjects to investors, it also found that discussion of strategy in annual reports fell from 84 percent to 62 percent between 1996 and 1998 (Mahoney, January 1999).

The Taylor survey also showed investor interest in a company's competitive position. While investors are looking for information about market share, competitors, and product/service comparisons, companies often provide only vague, general statements. Product information, which can indicate future market leadership, was rated third in importance in the Taylor survey. However, only 19 percent of companies provide useful information in this area (Mahoney, January 1999).

Previts et al. (1994) found that analysts address in their reports the quality of management, particularly after a management change. The Taylor survey (Mahoney, January 1999) reported that 68 percent of investors view information about management structure, credentials, and experience as very important. While 97 percent of U.S. companies describe their organizational structure, only 13 percent describe the business backgrounds of their key executives.

Conclusion

The literature supports the believed relevance ascribed to many specific content areas that are sometimes included in annual reports. However, the literature lacks sufficient descriptive work providing detailed information about what companies are actually including in annual reports. The present study is designed to offer a systematic examination of annual report contents, focusing on these areas of critical relevance to users

APPENDIX B

Research Methodology and Detailed Data

This is a study of the annual reports of 16 companies. The sample was selected to obtain a set of companies having characteristics satisfying the criteria outlined below. First we chose a set of target industries, listed in the left-hand column of table 1 (pages 2 and 3). These were identified from the "Standard & Poor's Listing by Industry Group" at the end of 1998. Our selection of the eight industries was designed to result in a diverse set of firms, and we therefore included industries as different as general retailing and chemicals. We sought to include consumer-oriented and industry-oriented industries, and industries in a variety of areas of the American economy. Although we believe that this procedure produced a representative set of industries, the choice of other industries might have yielded different results and insights.

We selected two relatively large firms to study in each industry. Because we focus on the contents of the annual reports, our sample is obtained from very large firms, the *Fortune* 500, as reported in 1998. These firms invest both attention and resources in investor relations and their annual reports. Therefore, these companies are appropriate to study as examples of state-of-the-art corporate communications.

Within the *Fortune* 500, we selected firms with significantly differing sales revenues to allow study of firms of varying sizes. However, even the smallest *Fortune* 500 firms are quite large. Our smallest company, Westvaco, which is ranked 472nd in sales revenues in the *Fortune* 500, has a market capitalization in excess of $3 billion. Column 8 in table 1 indicates the range of *Fortune* rankings in the sample. We devised a measure, rank of smaller divided by rank of larger, to measure the scale of the difference between the rankings of the pair of sample firms within each industry. This ratio ranges from 1.7 to 26.2, indicating that in the pair with the greatest difference, the rank of the smaller firm is 26 times that of the larger firm. Nevertheless, in only two industries (computer and electrical) is the smaller company's rank many times greater than the larger company's rank. Table 1 also reports the distribution of sample firms across the quintiles of the *Fortune* 500. Ten of the 16 firms are *Fortune* 100 companies, and in three industries (beverage, chemical, and retail) both firms selected were in the *Fortune* 100. In the computer and electrical industries, firms from the first and second 100 were included; the remaining three industries involved companies with larger differences in *Fortune* ranges.

In some cases, two companies within an industry are of similar sizes. For example, we paired Coca-Cola (#68) with PepsiCo (#31), and Sears (#16) with Wal-Mart (#4). In other industries, we selected two firms farther apart in their *Fortune* size ranks. For example, Westvaco (#472) and Champion (#277) were the choices in paper products, and Hershey (#345) and ConAgra (#45) were selected in foods. The market capitalization of the companies in the sample also ranges broadly, from $3.3 billion to $240 billion, with the total in the sample approaching $1 trillion.

When possible, we chose well-known firms in each industry. We also intentionally selected both more focused and more diversified companies. For example, Rockwell represents the former and General Electric the latter for our sample. We also intentionally picked companies that varied in the breadth of their product line, for example, ConAgra and Hershey in the food industry. In the computer area, we have one long-established company (IBM) and one comparatively younger company employing novel merchandising practices (Dell). In the paper products industry, we studied a relatively well-known manufacturer of many types of paper (Champion) and a niche manufacturer of paper containers (Westvaco). We provide information on the mission and profiles of these companies in appendix C. These materials, gathered from the Web sites of the firms, provide a succinct overview of how the sample companies see and describe themselves.

We studied two years, 1992 and 1997, obtaining and examining the reports these companies produced for both years. Selection of the same years for all firms allows better cross-sectional comparison because they all face a common economic environment. Particularly, we expect that two companies within an industry are likely to have faced similar economic conditions during the same time periods. We describe the most current year for which data were available when we began the project, and therefore selected the fiscal year incorporating 1997. Selecting 1992 as our earlier year allows for a five-year comparison with the 1997 report, and represents the year before the release of the tentative results of the AICPA Special Committee on Financial Reporting.

Table 2 presents additional, more current characteristics of the sample companies, including inside and institutional stockholders' ownership proportions, as reported in a 1999 *Market Guide*, and firm auditor as reported in the 1997 annual report.

Table 2
Sample Description, Shareholders' Information and Auditors (as reported in recent Market Guide *data, except auditor*)*

Company	Shares Outstanding *(in millions)*	Insider Ownership *(percent)*	Institutional Ownership *(percent)*	Auditor*
Champion	96	1.00	93.00	Arthur Andersen
Coca-Cola	2,465	14.00	51.75	Ernst & Young
ConAgra	488	2.00	55.65	Deloitte & Touche
Dell	1,274	17.00	50.13	Price Waterhouse
Dow	221	2.00	68.90	Deloitte & Touche
DuPont	1,126	2.00	53.49	Price Waterhouse
GE	3,268	<1.00	52.47	KPMG Peat Marwick
Hershey	143	<1.00	45.73	Arthur Andersen
IBM	923	<1.00	55.09	Price Waterhouse
Merck	1,191	<1.00	58.04	Arthur Andersen
PepsiCo	1,467	<1.00	59.46	KPMG Peat Marwick
Pharmacia & Upjohn	508	<1.00	73.31	Coopers & Lybrand
Rockwell	191	2.00	45.15	Deloitte & Touche
Sears	383	<1.00	82.91	Deloitte & Touche
Wal-Mart	2,253	41.00	41.01	Ernst & Young
Westvaco	100	4.00	72.52	Price Waterhouse

*As reported in 1997 annual report.

APPENDIX B

Institutional ownership varies widely, from 41 percent to 95 percent, exceeding 50 percent in 13 companies and 60 percent in 5 companies. Insider ownership ranges from less than 1 percent to 41 percent, but only three companies had insider holdings greater than 4 percent. While these characteristics were not criteria for our sample selection, they provide a possible basis for understanding some differences that we observe in reporting practice. All of the largest public accounting firms are represented in the most recent auditors of these companies' reports.

Additional summary information is presented in table 3 , including a description of the basic characteristics of each annual report. This table shows that there are many common elements within annual reports that are roughly comparable across companies in terms of length (number of pages) and placement in the report. The average number of pages in a report is 55; the president/CEO letter averages four of those pages; MD&A, eight pages; and GAAP-mandated information, 20 pages. All reports contain a mix of text and nontext presentations, and most include some significant graphical representations, particularly of specific financial statistics. Some companies in the sample used more visual representations, making greater use of pictures and color.

Our review of the literature suggests that the nonmandated information may be particularly important. Our review of the annual reports focused on those content areas that were likely to yield information above and beyond what can be found in the financial statements stipulated by GAAP, specifically president/CEO's letter, MD&A, and other narrative materials.

The focus of this study is the nonfinancial performance indicators and operating measures included by companies in their annual reports. To assess the occurrence of these items in company annual reports, we studied the annual report contents of each sample company. We classified the information items found within each company's annual report into the following categories (see table 4 for an abbreviated version of the detailed coding document):

A. Corporate Structure
B. Description of Business and Properties
C. Investor Information
D. Personnel Information

Table 3
Physical Characteristics of Annual Reports

Company	Report Year	Size	CEO Letter	MD&A	GAAP Content	Percent with Visual Content	Visual Content Financial	Components Nonfinancial
		pages	*pages*	*pages*	*pages*	*percent*	*percent*	*percent*
Champion	97	62	4	8	21	73	55	45
	92	58	6	6	22	57	76	24
Coca-Cola	97	68	6	9	22	85	50	50
	92	74	11	8	22	85	58	42
ConAgra	98	74	2	7	21	81	51	49
	93	54	3	4	18	84	58	42
Dell	98	54	5	5	19	78	58	42
	93	42	5	8	14	68	74	26
Dow	97	52	4	12	16	84	74	26
	92	54	3	11	24	78	78	22
DuPont	97	66	3	14	32	68	74	26
	92	66	3	6	31	82	71	29
GE	97	68	6	14	27	80	71	29
	92	64	5	12	25	84	65	35
Hershey	97	44	*	*	*	55	69	31
	92	42	2	7	15	76	53	47
IBM	97	82	8	10	29	80	54	46
	92	74	5	6	27	49	64	36
Merck	97	60	2	10	15	78	46	53
	92	50	2	7	13	89	47	53
PepsiCo	97	38	11	8	15	8[illegible]	76	24
	92	54	4	20	15	8[illegible]	76	24
Pharmacia & Upjohn	97	58	4	8	21	7[illegible]	57	43
	92	54	4	7	20	5[illegible]	69	31
Rockwell	97	50	5	9	*	64	25	75
	92	38	2	4	14	82	65	35
Sears	97	46	2	7	16	83	54	46
	92	58	3	9	25	85	80	20
Wal-Mart	97	38	2	3	12	94	36	64
	92	22	2	2	13	70	81	19
Westvaco	97	38	3	4	18	84	50	50
	92	34	4	3	16	57	69	31

*Some form of summary report.

E. Production and Products
F. Forward-Looking and Future-Oriented Information
G. Marketing
H. Relationships with Other Parties
I. Industry Information
J. Nonmandated Financial Information (including segment level data)
K. Strategic Planning

Corporate structure refers to the most general characteristics of the company, and may indicate both historical characteristics and future potential as represented by size, board activity, and existing subsidiaries. **Description of business and properties** provides information about the company's productive assets and their deployment. It incorporates, among other things, physical plant issues, geographical dispersion, and the existence of expansion activities. **Investor information** is composed

Table 4
Coding Form, Abbreviated Version

		Location		
		MD&A	Pres. Let.	Other
	Company Name Overall orientation of report Type of report			
Category Label	**Category Name**			
A	**Corporate structure** subsidiaries description size statistics (number of stores, etc.) history (timeline, key events, etc.) culture, mission, values mergers & acquisitions activity			
B	**Description of business and properties** locations, openings, development rankings (*Forbes*, *Fortune*, etc.) productive capacity, expansion line of business breakdowns geographic breakdowns			

Table 4
Coding Form, Abbreviated Version (Continued)

		Location		
		MD&A	Pres. Let.	Other
C	**Investor information** shareholder information change in investor composition accessibility information (e.g., investor relations phone numbers)			
D	**Personnel information** employment and compensation data information on officers and board members training/development policies			
E	**Production and products** description (text or pictures), use product strategies, introductions, phaseouts, mix production cycle and costs transportation and logistics quality initiatives and recognitions (e.g., ISO 9000) patents attained service enhancements/innovation backlogs			
F	**Forward-looking and future-oriented information** projected financial statements future strategies future performance targets future marketing plans future growth (locations, etc.) anticipated mergers/acquisitions business risk			
G	**Marketing** key customers, clients new promotional efforts competitive position analysis new markets entered			

Table 4
Coding Form, Abbreviated Version (Continued)

		Location		
		MD&A	Pres. Let.	Other
H	**Relationships with other parties** environmental (pollution, packaging, emissions, recycling) safety issues (education, workers' comp, public) code of conduct or ethics customer relationships and satisfaction joint ventures regulatory changes litigation results community relationships and charitable giving			
I	**Industry information** industry product demand and price trend marketplace opportunities and comparisons market share—overall market share—product segment market share—geographic			
J	**Nonmandated financial information** graphics, charts, time series, etc. ratios (PE, market cap, div. yield) stock price history, volume other investment information (S & P, web links, analyst report) segment details (volume, profitability, investment) dividend history and trend cash flow history stock repurchases and impact hedging activities and results			
K	**Strategic planning** growth strategies systems and technology plans research and development initiatives current company general strategies benchmarking plans			

of disclosures specifically relevant to shareholders, including stock price performance and shareholder returns. **Personnel information** includes such items as workforce characteristics, employment statistics, incentive compensation issues, and training and development policies. **Production and products** incorporates all product-specific text, including such items as descriptions, introductions, costs, quality initiatives, patents, and production cycle information. **Forward-looking and future-oriented information** contains disclosures bearing on companies' future performance. This category covers both specific and general materials pertaining to future performance, including such information as performance targets, anticipated mergers, expected capital expenditures, and projected financial information.

The **marketing** category includes information about marketing priorities, pursuit of key customers, and current product demand. Performance in this sense is reflected in how a company sees itself managing its selling opportunities. **Relationships with other parties** includes strategic relationships with other producers and customers, environmental and safety issues, regulatory issues, community relationships, and charitable giving. **Industry information** includes industry outlooks and statistics and market economic factors. This information reflects the company's performance as part of the general environment.

The **nonmandated financial information** category includes various nonmandated operating measures or derivatives thereof (e.g., ratios), including segment details, information time series, specific performance measures such as EBITDA or free cash flow, and other financial measures that are not part of mandated GAAP. This information presents traditional and nontraditional disclosures that often address performance issues about the company. Finally, **strategic planning** incorporates discussions of company strategies. These could be general company-level strategies or specific goals, such as a plan for the marketing of particular products to specific types of customers.

These categories provide structure and perspective for the data analysis. To determine nonrequired information disclosed, two to three researchers read each of the 32 annual reports in full and in detail. Based on pilot studies, we developed a coding instrument to help categorize the large volume of data in the reports into the above 11 categories (see table 4). The information was organized into these categories by location within the report. The possible locations for information within the annual report were identified as follows:

President's/CEO's letter

MD&A

Other narrative sections

Notes to financial statements

Our preliminary reading of several annual reports suggested that little information pertinent to this study was contained in the notes section. The close association between the notes and the financial statements is such that the contents of the notes are principally required disclosures related to the financial statements. Accordingly, the scope of this project focused on the remaining three sections. Nonetheless, we continued to review the notes section for exceptional information.

After an annual report was read and coded, a preliminary analysis of the company's annual reports was drafted. The write-ups and the coding forms were compared by the individual readers, and significant differences were reconciled. Then a revised analysis was prepared and reviewed. The following discussion summarizes the coding output.

Because we employ a case study method, our analysis generally avoids explicit comparisons. We focus instead on describing the content of individual company annual reports. Nevertheless, as described above, some comparisons are conducted, where pertinent, involving companies within individual industries, and for individual companies across time periods. The following tables and figures present the more detailed results of the coding process. In these tables and charts, the definitions of the coding categories are as presented above. The proportions presented are calculated as the number of coded items in a category divided by the total number of coded items in an annual report. In these tables the companies and their industries have been randomly presented to preserve anonymity.

Table 5 presents the maximum and minimum individual company proportions of coded items in each category A–K. This table suggests a diversity in approaches to annual report disclosure. For example, Category J ranges from 40 percent to 11 percent, while category C ranges from 4 percent to 0 percent. Table 6 and figure 1 compare the propor-

Table 5
Maximum and Minimum Proportions (by Individual Company) in Each Coding Category Totaled across Both Years

Description	Category	Max	Min
Corporate Structure	A	0.13	0.01
Description of Business and Properties	B	0.27	0.01
Investor Information	C	0.04	0.00
Personnel Information	D	0.08	0.00
Production and Products	E	0.39	0.08
Forward-Looking and Future-Oriented Information	F	0.19	0.03
Marketing	G	0.08	0.00
Relationships with Other Parties	H	0.20	0.01
Industry Information	I	0.18	0.01
Nonmandated Financial Information	J	0.40	0.11
Strategic Planning	K	0.12	0.01

tions and numbers of coded items between the years 1992 and 1997. Table 6 presents the average proportions (across all companies) coded by category in each year, and the change between the years. Coding properties are relatively consistent between the two years; the largest change is a drop of 5 percent in category J. Figure 1 presents similar information as a bar chart. The shaded bars are 1992 information. This graphically confirms the consistency in the proportions and the raw numbers across the two years.

Figures 2a and 2b provide a more detailed elaboration of the preceding information, where 2a presents 1992 and 2b presents 1997 detailed coding results. These charts present coding in each category for each of the 16 companies, randomly assigned numbers 1 to 16. These figures illustrate the similarities and differences among companies across categories. For example, the proportions of coded items appearing in categories C and D are low for most companies in 1992 and remain

APPENDIX B

Table 6
Average Proportions across All Companies Coded into Each Category, by Year

Description	Category	1992	1997	Change*
Corporate Structure	A	0.05	0.07	0.02
Description of Business and Properties	B	0.09	0.10	0.01
Investor Information	C	0.02	0.02	0.00
Personnel Information	D	0.03	0.05	0.02
Production and Products	E	0.20	0.19	-0.01
Forward-Looking and Future-Oriented Information	F	0.08	0.08	-0.01
Marketing	G	0.04	0.05	0.01
Relationships with Other Parties	H	0.09	0.10	0.01
Industry Information	I	0.07	0.07	0.00
Nonmandated Financial Information	J	0.29	0.24	-0.05
Strategic Planning	K	0.04	0.04	-0.01

*Change column is affected by rounding.

low in 1997. On the other hand, for most companies, categories E and J provide most of the coded items in both years. Nevertheless, there are exceptions, such as company 9, which has a lower proportion than most companies in category E and a higher proportion in category B.

Figure 3 illustrates comparisons within industries, again preserving individual anonymity. The industries have been assigned designations a to h, with lettering assigned in random order. These eight charts present the coding proportions for the two companies within each industry (designated Companies Y and Z) to illustrate where industry similarities may exist. There are some differences in all industries because all companies are unique, but industries "b" and "h" provide examples of similar profiles for coded items. In contrast, for example, in industry "a," one company provides more information from category B than the other from the same industry provides.

Figure 1
1992–1997 Comparison of Disclosures by Categories

These charts compare the average proportion of coded items and the average number of coded items across the two years.

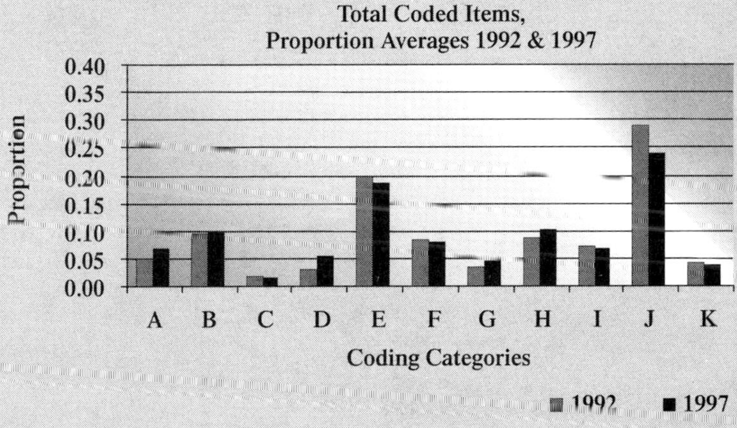

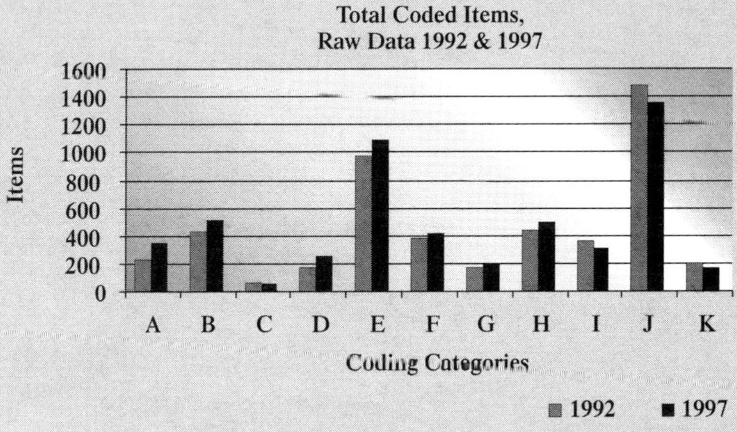

Figure 2a
1992 Coding Category Proportions across Companies
(Intercompany Comparisons)

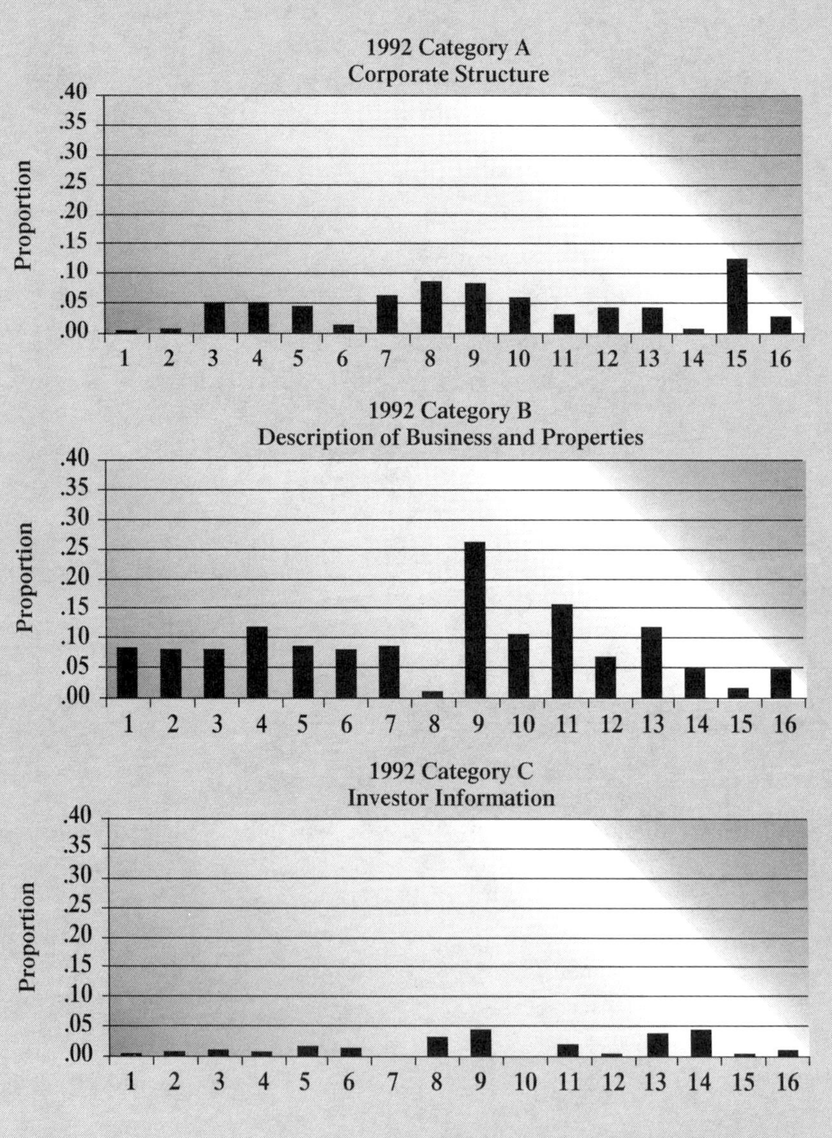

Figure 2a
1992 Coding Category Proportions across Companies
(Intercompany Comparisons) *(Continued)*

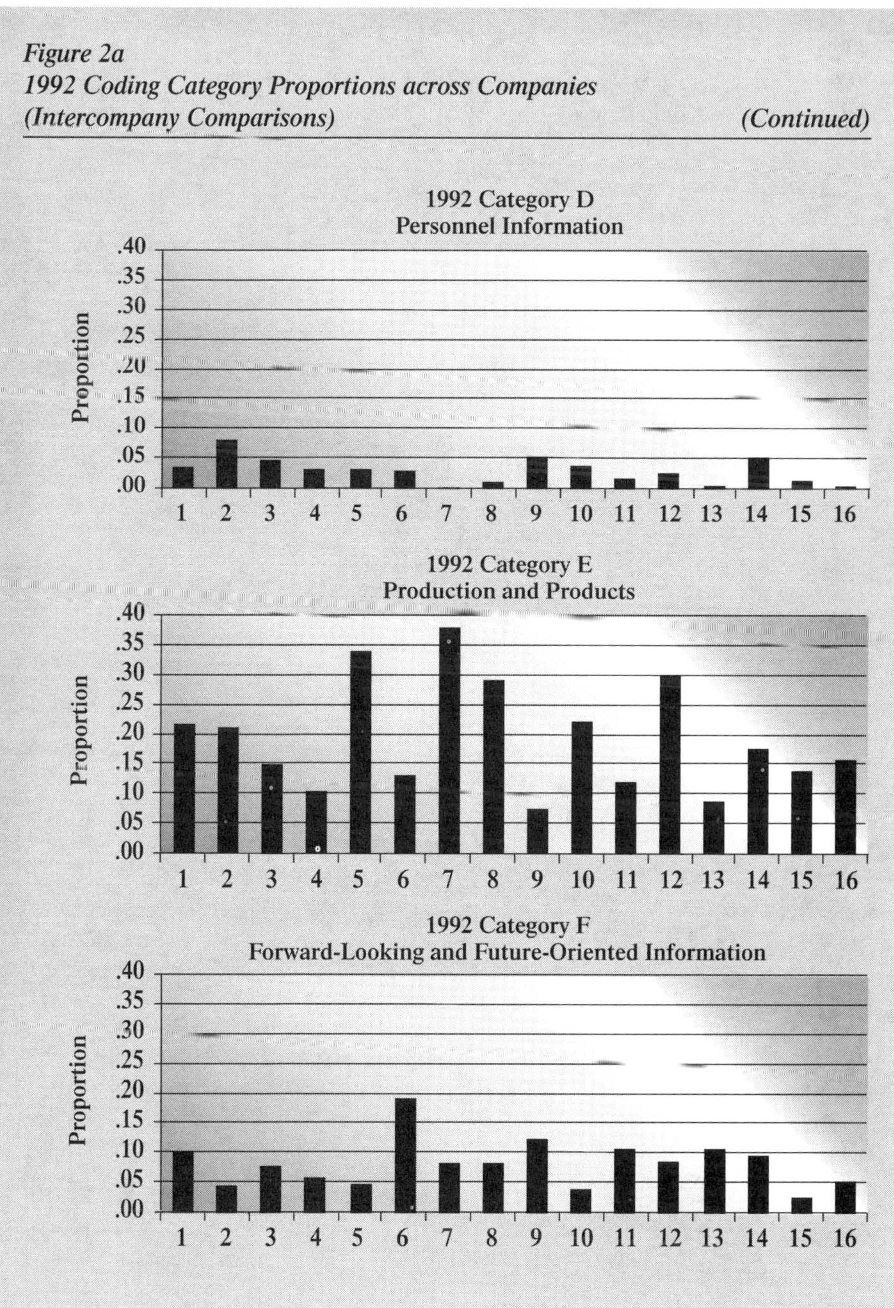

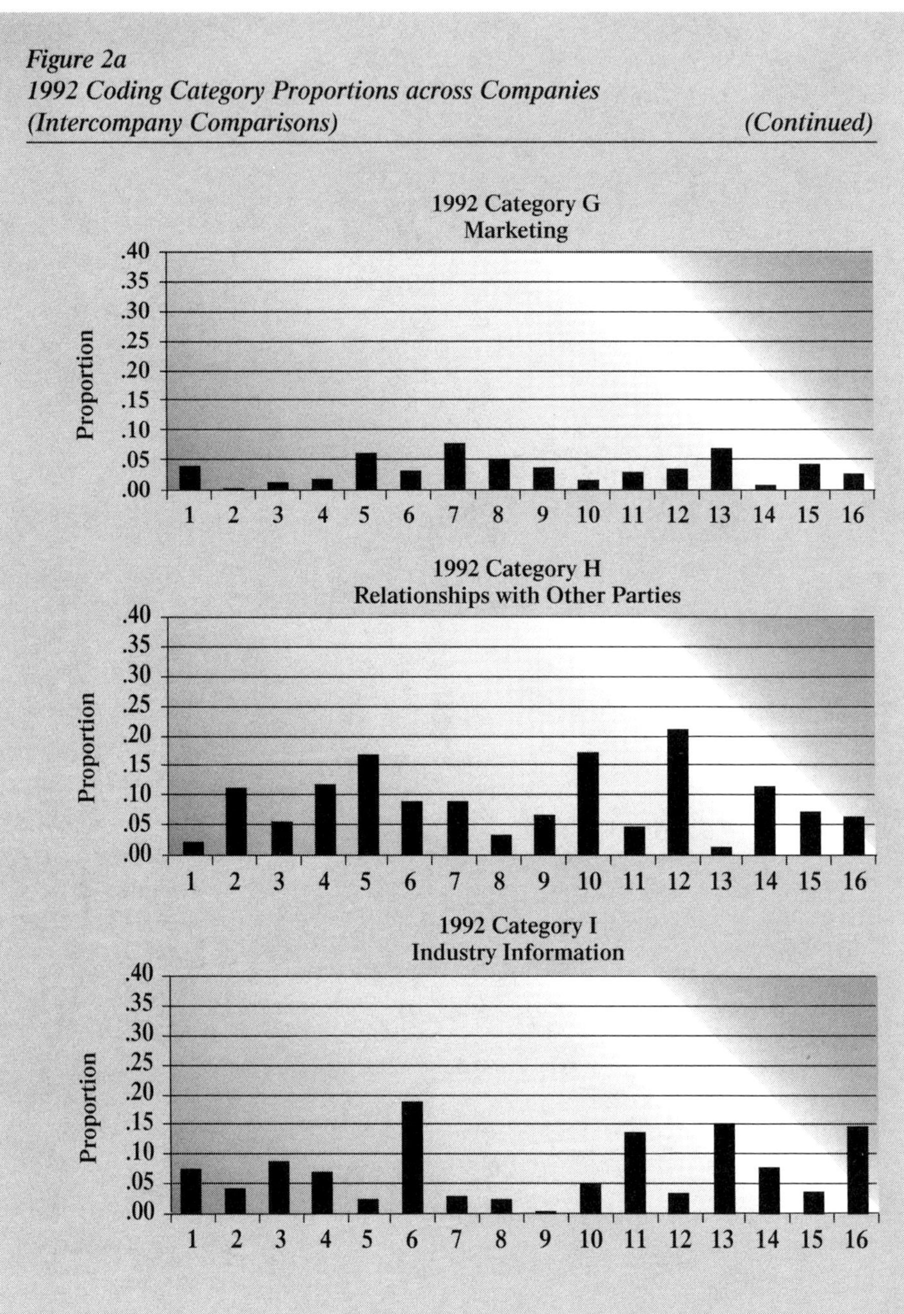

Figure 2a
1992 Coding Category Proportions across Companies
(Intercompany Comparisons) *(Continued)*

Figure 2a
1992 Coding Category Proportions across Companies
(Intercompany Comparisons) *(Continued)*

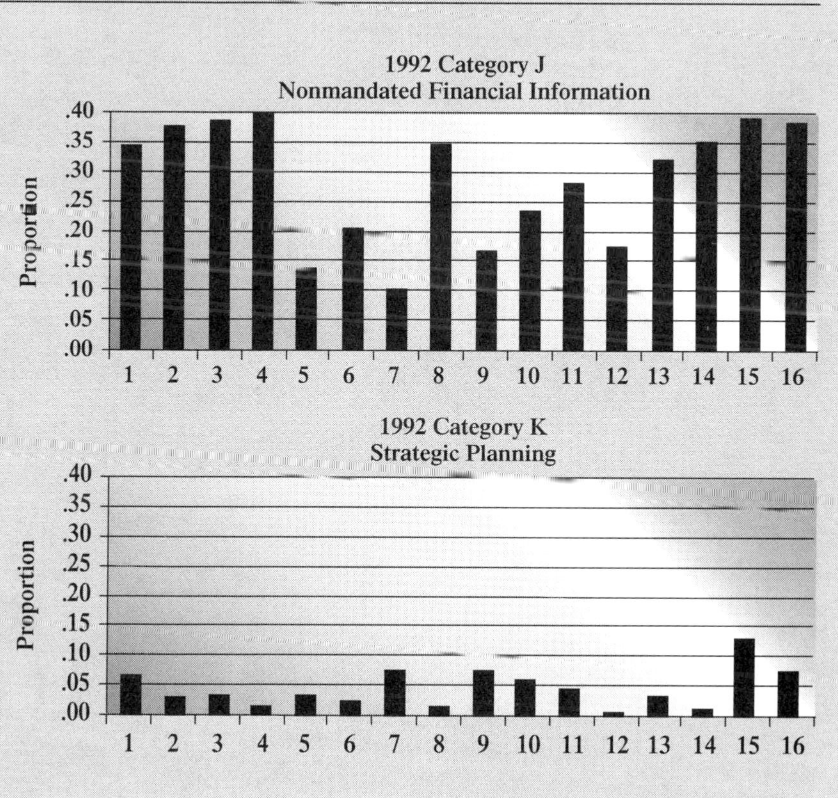

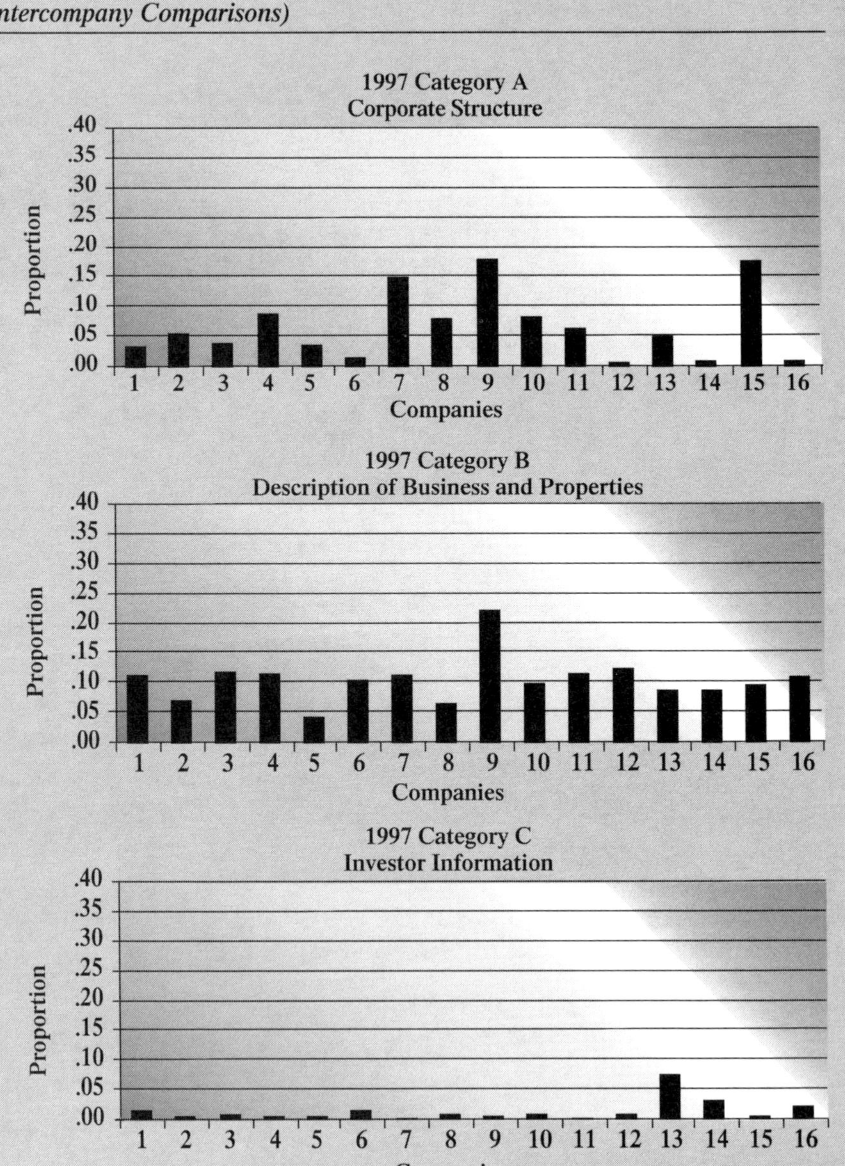
Figure 2b
1997 Coding Category Proportions across Companies
(Intercompany Comparisons)
1997 Category A
Corporate Structure
Proportion
.40
.35
.30
.25
.20
.15
.10
.05
.00
1 2 3 4 5 6 7 8 9 10 11 12 13 14 15 16
Companies
1997 Category B
Description of Business and Properties
Proportion
.40
.35
.30
.25
.20
.15
.10
.05
.00
1 2 3 4 5 6 7 8 9 10 11 12 13 14 15 16
Companies
1997 Category C
Investor Information
Proportion
.40
.35
.30
.25
.20
.15
.10
.05
.00
1 2 3 4 5 6 7 8 9 10 11 12 13 14 15 16
Companies

Figure 2b
1997 Coding Category Proportions across Companies
(Intercompany Comparisons) *(Continued)*

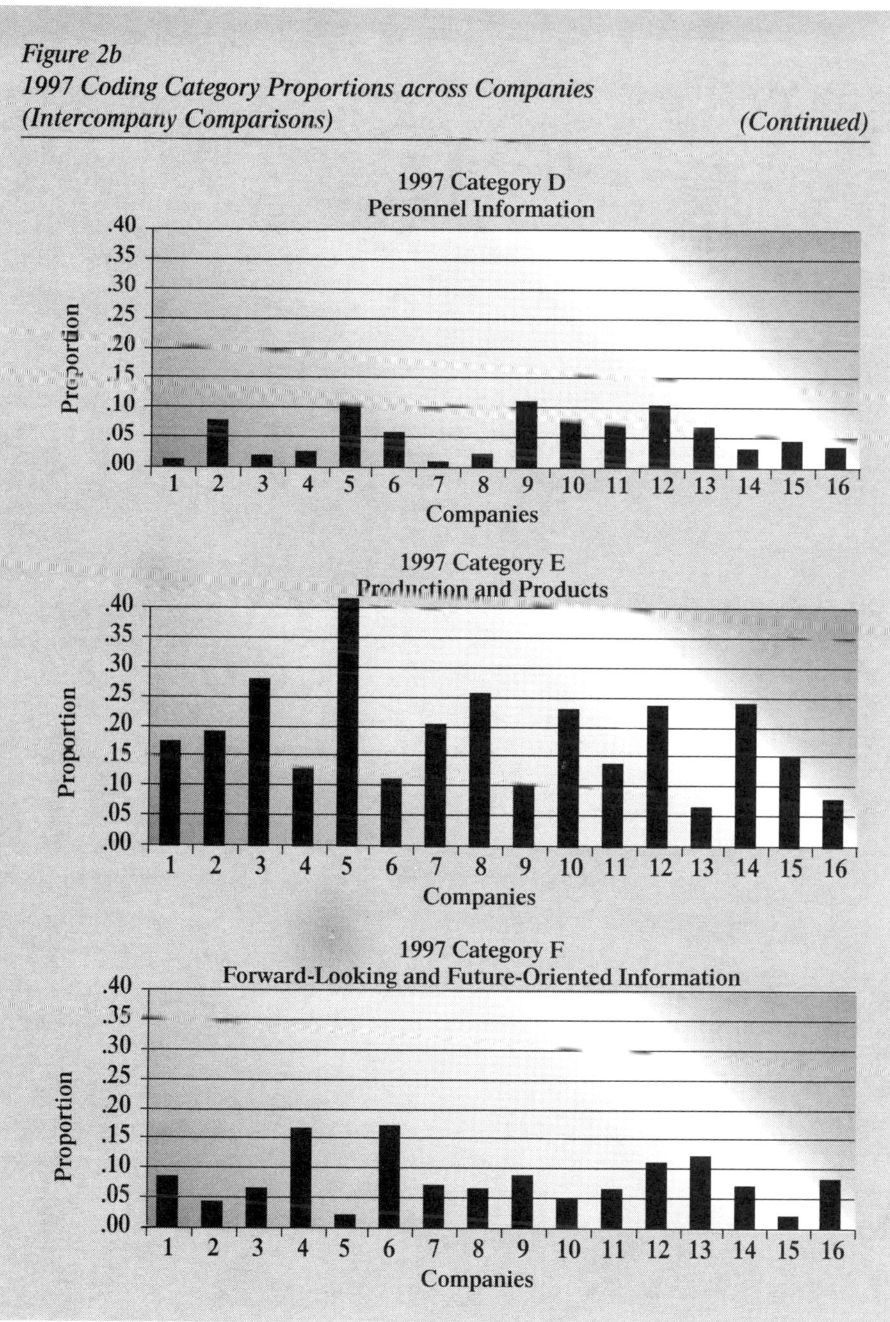

Figure 2b
1997 Coding Category Proportions across Companies
(Intercompany Comparisons) *(Continued)*

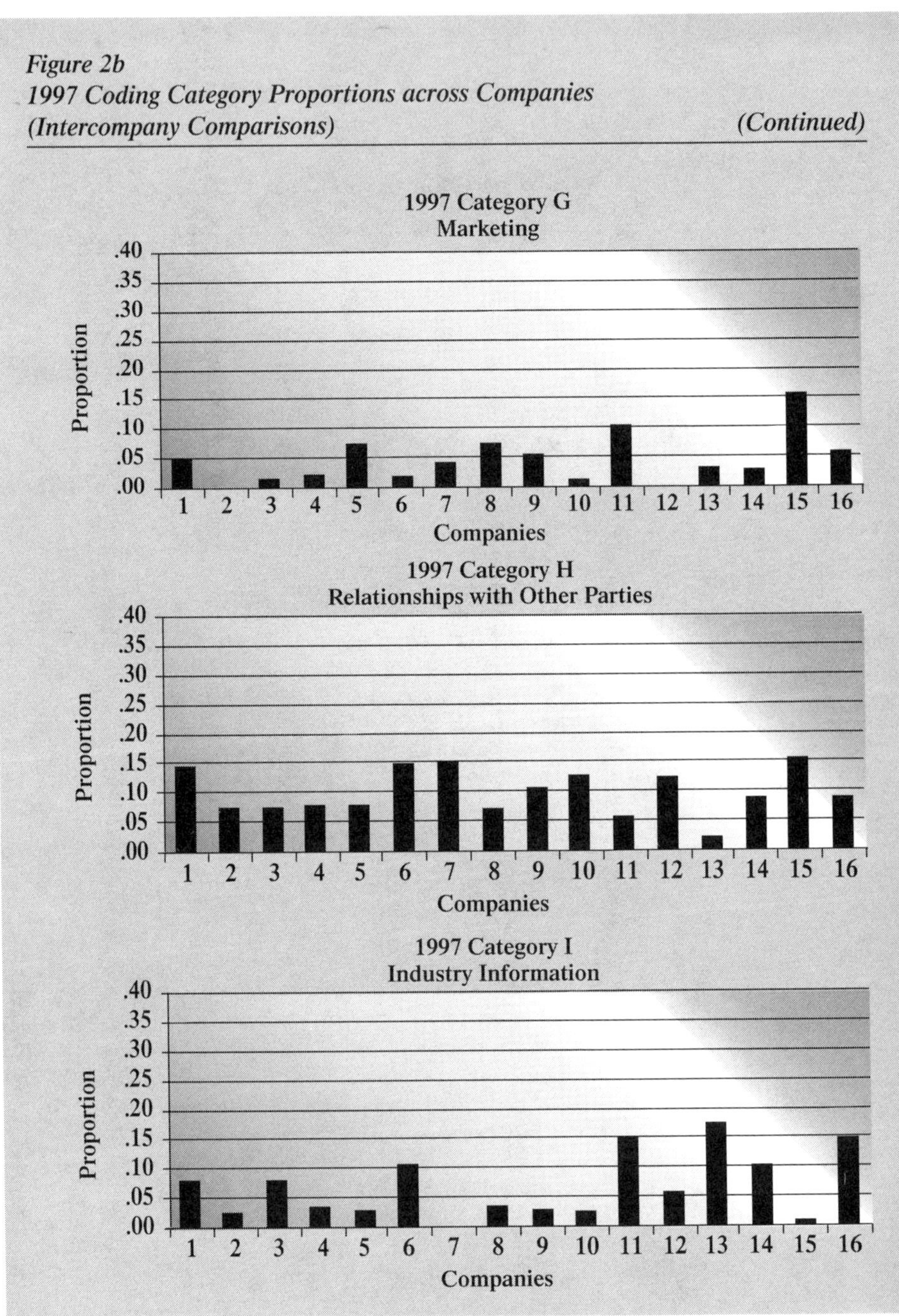

Figure 2b
1997 Coding Category Proportions across Companies
(Intercompany Comparisons) *(Continued)*

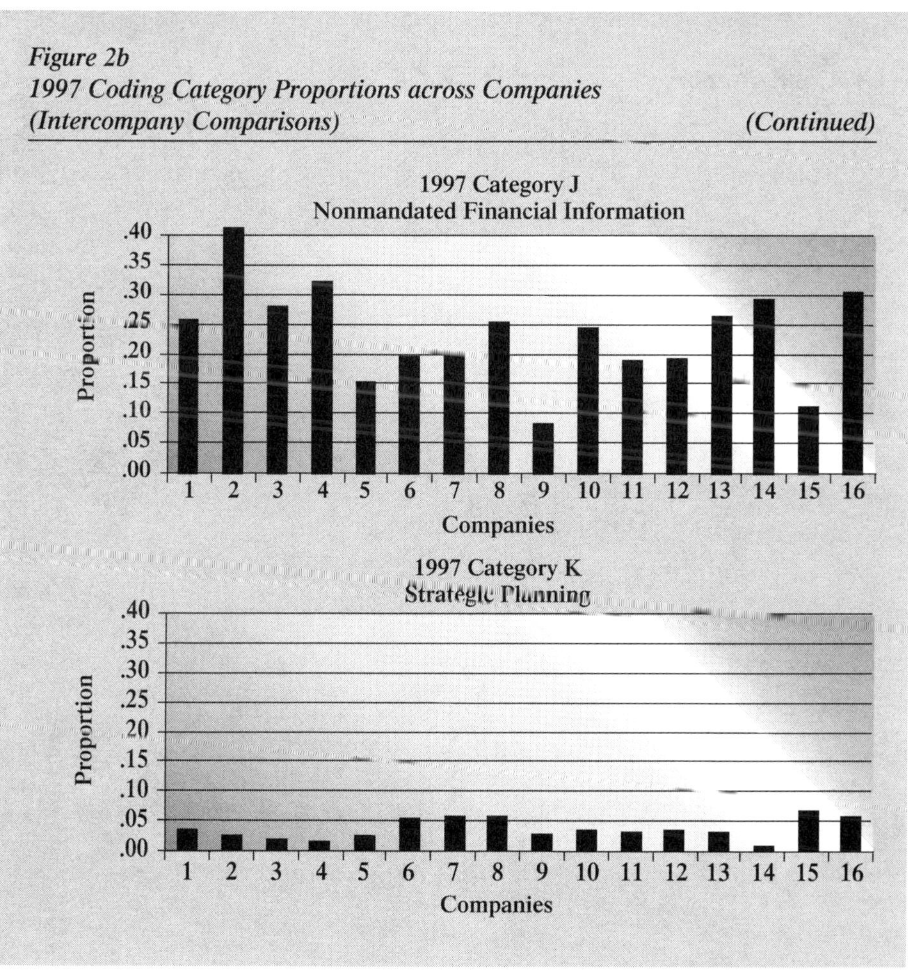

APPENDIX B

Figure 3
Intra-Industry Comparisons of Coding Category Proportions

These charts compare two companies within the same industry, based on the proportions of total coded items across both years in each coding category A-K.

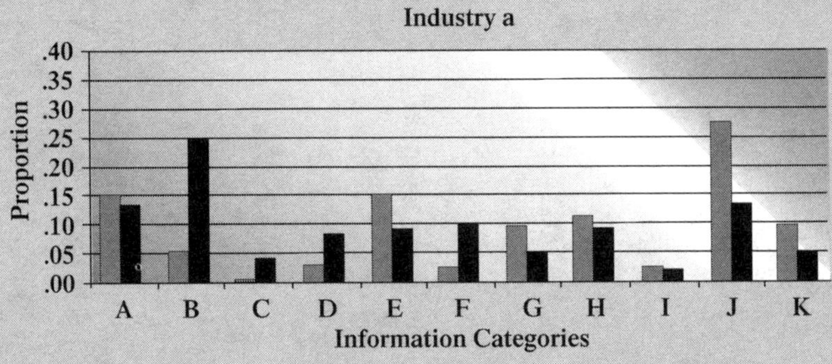

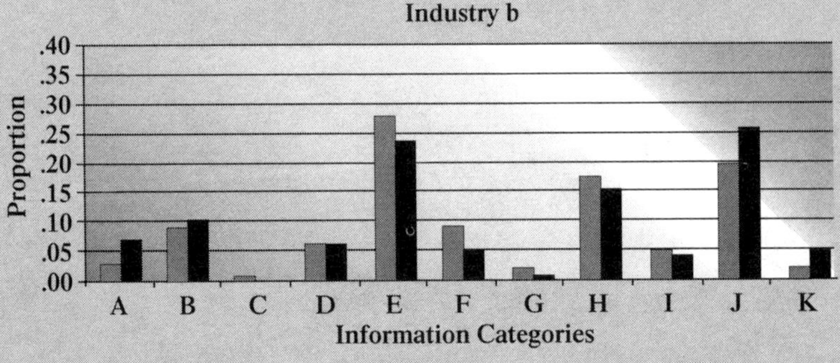

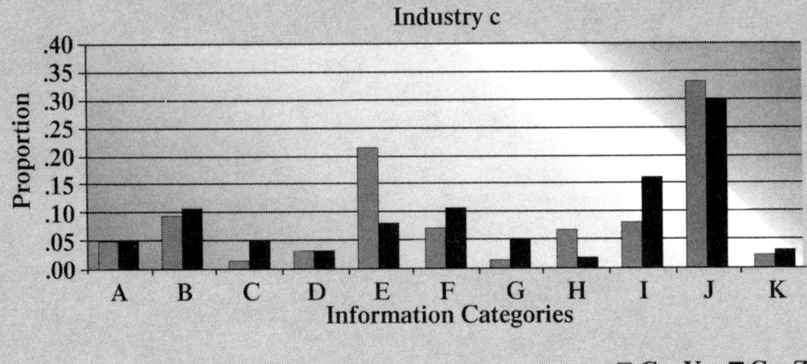

Figure 3
Intra-Industry Comparisons of Coding Category Proportions *(Continued)*

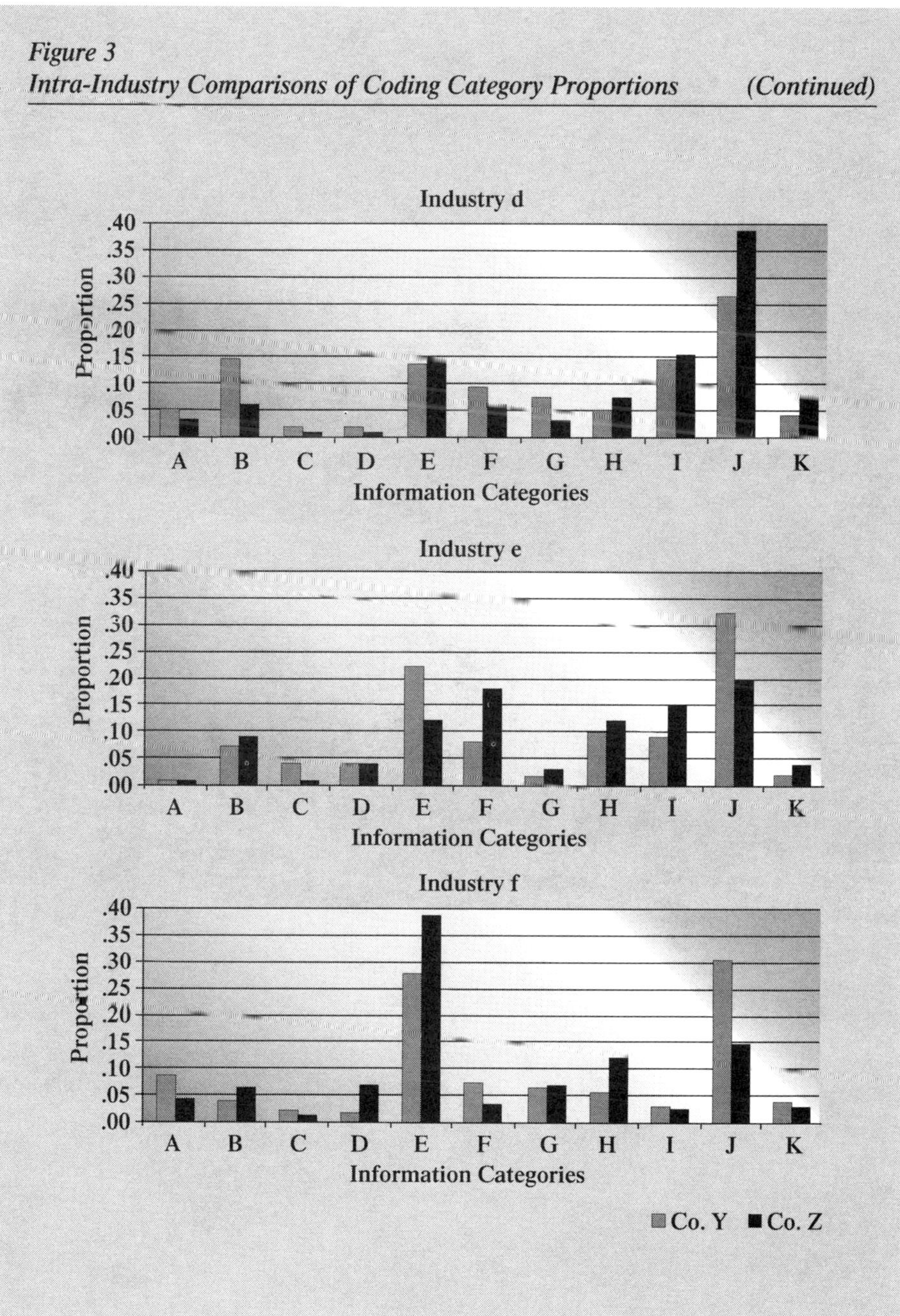

Figure 3
Intra-Industry Comparisons of Coding Category Proportions *(Continued)*

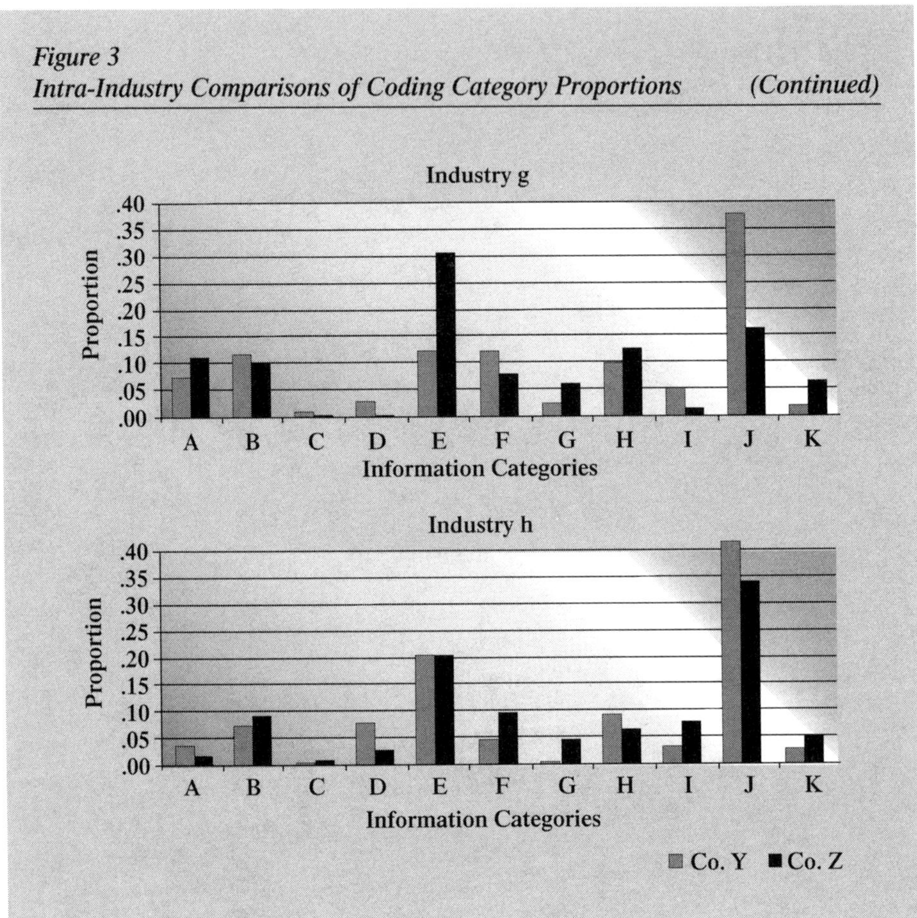

APPENDIX C

Company Background Information

The mission, values, and profiles of the companies selected for study are quoted or paraphrased/summarized below, **as described on each company's Web site during 1999.** Web site addresses are provided for further reference.

Champion International Corporation

www.championpaper.com

Mission

Champion's objective is leadership in the American industry. Profitable growth is fundamental to the achievement of that goal and will benefit all to whom we are responsible: shareholders, customers, employees, communities, and society at large.

Champion's way of achieving profitable growth requires the active participation of all employees in increasing productivity, reducing costs, improving quality, and strengthening customer service.

...Champion believes that only through the individual actions of all employees—guided by a company-wide commitment to excellence—will our long-term economic success and leadership position be ensured.

Profile

Champion, one of our nation's leading manufacturers of paper for business, communications, commercial printing, publication papers, and newspapers, employs 18,000 persons in facilities across the United States. Champion, a major producer of lumber and plywood, has roots which reach back to the 1890s, when the Champion Coated Paper Company was founded in Hamilton, Ohio. In 1906, the Champion Fibre Company was formed to provide pulp for the Champion Coated

Paper Company. The two companies merged in 1935 to form The Champion Paper and Fibre Company, later Champion Papers Inc.

Over the years, the company grew, adding paper mills and other businesses. In 1967, Champion Papers Inc. merged with a huge plywood and lumber manufacturer—United States Plywood Corporation—to form U.S. Plywood-Champion Papers Inc. The company became Champion International Corporation in 1972, adding a major packaging business with the purchase of Hoerner Waldorf Corporation in 1977. The 1984 merger of Champion International with St. Regis Corporation put the company into the publication papers and newsprint businesses, making Champion a major producer of both coated and uncoated groundwood papers. This merger doubled the amount of timberland owned or controlled, making Champion one of the largest private landowners in the United States.

The Coca-Cola Company

www.coke.com

Mission

We exist to create value for our share owners on a long-term basis by building a business that enhances The Coca-Cola Company's trademarks. This also is our ultimate commitment. As the world's largest beverage company, we refresh that world. We do this by developing superior soft drinks, both carbonated and noncarbonated, and profitable nonalcoholic beverage systems that create value for our Company, our bottling partners, our customers, our share owners and the communities in which we do business.

Profile

The Coca-Cola Company is the global soft-drink industry leader, with world headquarters in Atlanta, Georgia. The Company and its subsidiaries employ nearly 30,000 people around the world. Syrups, concentrates and beverage bases for Coca-Cola, the Company's flagship brand, and over 160 other Company soft-drink brands are manufactured and sold by The Coca-Cola Company and its subsidiaries in nearly 200 countries around the world. In fact, approximately 70 percent of Company volume and 80 percent of Company profit come from outside the United States.

ConAgra, Inc.

www.conagra.com

Mission

ConAgra is a diversified international food company. We operate across the food chain, in 35 countries around the world. Our mission is to increase stockholders' wealth. Our job is to help feed people better.

ConAgra people are committed to achieving premium results. We pride ourselves on our success in serving our customers and meeting consumer needs.

Profile

ConAgra is the food industry leader in consistent, strong long-term earnings growth. (ConAgra's 18 consecutive years of earnings per share growth at a compound rate of 15 percent is unequaled by any major food company in the United States, and probably the world.) ConAgra employs 82,000 persons.

Of 70+ ConAgra brands, 25 each chalk up annual retail sales exceeding $100 million: Act II, Armour, Banquet, Blue Bonnet, Butterball, Cook's, Country Pride, County Line, Decker, Eckrich, Fleischmann's, Healthy Choice, Hebrew National, Hunt's, Hunt's Snack Pack, La Choy, Marie Callender's, Orville Redenbacher's, Parkay, Peter Pan, Slim Jim, Swift Premium, Swiss Miss, Van Camp's and Wesson.

APPENDIX C

Dell Computer Corporation

www.dell.com

Mission

Dell's mission is to be the most successful computer company in the world at delivering the best customer experience in markets we serve. In doing so, Dell will meet customer expectations of:

- Highest quality
- Leading technology
- Competitive pricing
- Individual and company accountability
- Best-in-class service and support
- Flexible customization capability
- Superior corporate citizenship
- Financial stability

Profile

At the heart of its performance is Dell's unique direct-to-customer business model. "Direct" refers to the company's relationships with its customers, from home-PC users to the world's largest corporations. There are no retailers or other resellers adding unnecessary time and cost, or diminishing Dell's understanding of customer expectations

By taking its direct business model to even higher levels, through the Internet and value-added services, Dell intends to continue to grow its business at a multiple of the high-growth rate anticipated for the computer-systems industry as a whole.

The Dow Chemical Company

www.dow.com

Mission

To be the most productive, best value-growth chemical company in the world. To be the best at applying chemistry to benefit customers, employees, shareholders and society.

Fundamental to our success are the Values we believe in and practice.

People are the source of our success. We treat one another with respect, promote teamwork, and encourage personal freedom and growth. Leadership and excellence in performance are sought and rewarded.

Customers are the reason we exist. They receive our strongest commitment to meet their needs. Our Products and Services reflect dedication to quality, innovation and value.

Our Conduct demonstrates integrity and commitment to ethics, safety, health and the environment.

Profile

The Dow Chemical Company is a global science and technology based company that develops and manufactures a portfolio of chemical, plastic and agricultural products and services for customers in 168 countries around the world. With annual sales of more than $18 billion, Dow conducts its operations through 14 global businesses. The company has 121 manufacturing sites in 32 countries and supplies more than 3,500 products.

The 39,000 Dow people around the world develop solutions for society based on Dow's inherent strength in science and technology—which we refer to as "good thinking." Good thinking helps customers succeed, stockholders prosper, employees achieve and communities thrive.

APPENDIX C

E.I. du Pont de Nemours and Company

www.dupont.com

Mission

We, the people of DuPont, dedicate ourselves daily to the work of improving life on our planet.

We have the curiosity to go farther...the imagination to think bigger...the determination to try harder...and the conscience to care more.

Our solutions will be bold. We will answer the fundamental needs of the people we live with to ensure harmony, health and prosperity in the world.

Our methods will be our obsession. Our singular focus will be to serve humanity with the power of all the sciences available to us.

Our tools are our minds. We will encourage unconventional ideas, be daring in our thinking, and courageous in our actions. By sharing our knowledge and learning from each other and the markets we serve, we will solve problems in surprising and magnificent ways.

Our success will be ensured. We will be demanding of ourselves and work relentlessly to complete our tasks. Our achievements will create superior profit for our shareholders and ourselves.

Our principles are sacred. We will respect nature and living things, work safely, be gracious to one another and our partners, and each day we will leave for home with consciences clear and spirits soaring.

Profile

DuPont is a science company, delivering science-based solutions that make a difference in people's lives in food and nutrition; health care; apparel; home and construction; electronics; and transportation. Founded in 1802, the company operates in 65 countries and has 92,000 employees.

General Electric Company

www.ge.com

Mission

GE's Mission Statement is developed through its Management Values, which are expressed in the following statements.

GE Leaders, Always with Unyielding Integrity:

- Have a passion for excellence and hate bureaucracy
- Are open to ideas from anywhere and committed to Work Out
- Live quality and drive cost and speed for competitive advantage
- Have the self-confidence to involve everyone and behave in a boundaryless fashion
- Create a clear, simple, reality-based vision and communicate it to all constituencies
- Have enormous energy and the ability to energize others
- Stretch, set aggressive goals and reward progress, yet understand accountability and commitment
- See change as opportunity, not a threat
- Have global brains and build diverse and global teams

Profile

GE traces its beginnings to Thomas A. Edison, who established the Edison Electric Light Company in 1878. In 1892, a merger of the Edison General Electric Company and the Thomson-Houston Electric Company created General Electric Company. GE is the only company listed in the Dow Jones Industrial Index today that was also included in the original index in 1896. The company is a diversified services, technology, and manufacturing company with a commitment to achieving worldwide leadership in each of its businesses. GE operates in more than 100 countries around the world. GE employs 293,000 people worldwide, including 163,000 in the United States. GE has over 2.1 million shareowners. John F. Welch has been Chairman and Chief Executive Officer of GE since 1981.

Hershey Foods Corporation

www.hersheys.com

Mission

To be a focused food company in North America and selected international markets and a leader in every aspect of our business. Our goal is to enhance our number one position in the North American confectionery market, be the leader in chocolate-related grocery products, and build leadership positions in selected international markets.

Profile

Hershey Foods Corporation and its subsidiaries are engaged in the manufacture, distribution and sale of consumer food products. The Corporation, through its Hershey Chocolate North America and Hershey International divisions, produces and distributes a broad line of chocolate and non-chocolate confectionery and grocery products. Hershey is currently the U.S. market leader in both chocolate and non-chocolate confectionery.

The Corporation's principal product groups include: chocolate and non-chocolate confectionery products sold in the form of bar goods, bagged items and boxed items; grocery products in the form of baking ingredients, chocolate drink mixes, peanut butter, dessert toppings and beverages. The Corporation believes it is a major factor in these product groups in North America.

International Business Machines Corporation

www.ibm.com

Mission

At IBM, we strive to lead in the creation, development and manufacture of the industry's most advanced information technologies, including computer systems, software, networking systems, storage devices and microelectronics. We translate these advanced technologies into value for our customers through our professional solutions and services businesses worldwide.

Profile

Number of employees (1998): 291,067
Number of common stock holders (1998): 616,800
IBM's strategic vision is a networked world that transforms the way people work, interact, learn and do business.

Merck & Co., Inc.

www.merck.com

Mission

The mission of Merck is to provide society with superior products and services—innovations and solutions that improve the quality of life and satisfy customer needs—to provide employees with meaningful work and advancement opportunities and investors with a superior rate of return.

"We try never to forget that medicine is for the people. It is not for the profits. The profits follow, and if we have remembered that, they have never failed to appear." *George W. Merck*

Profile

Merck & Co., Inc. is a leading research-driven pharmaceutical products and services company. Merck discovers, develops, manufactures and markets a broad range of innovative products to improve human and animal health. The Merck-Medco Managed Care Division manages pharmacy benefits for more than 40 million Americans, encouraging the appropriate use of medicines and providing disease management programs.

PepsiCo, Inc.

www.pepsico.com

Mission

PepsiCo's overall mission is to increase the value of our shareholder's investment. We do this through sales growth, cost controls and wise investment of resources. We believe our commercial success depends upon offering quality and value to our consumers and customers; providing products that are safe, wholesome, economically efficient and environmentally sound; and providing a fair return to our investors while adhering to the highest standards of integrity.

Profile

PepsiCo, Inc. is among the most successful consumer products companies in the world, with 1998 revenues of over $22 billion and 151,000 employees. The company consists of: Pepsi-Cola Company, the world's second largest beverage company; Frito-Lay Company, the world's largest manufacturer and distributor of snack chips and Tropicana Products, Inc., the world's largest marketer and producer of branded juices. PepsiCo's brand names are among the best known and most respected in the world.

Some of PepsiCo's brand names are 100 years old, but the corporation is relatively young. PepsiCo, Inc. was founded in 1965 through the merger of Pepsi-Cola and Frito-Lay. Tropicana was acquired in 1998.

PepsiCo's success is the result of superior products, high standards of performance, distinctive competitive strategies and the high integrity of our people.

Our overriding objective is to increase the value of our shareholders' investment through integrated operating, investing and financing activities. Our strategy is to concentrate our resources on growing our businesses, both through internal growth and carefully selected acquisitions. Our strategy is continually fine-tuned to address the opportunities and risks of the global marketplace. The corporation's success reflects our continuing commitment to growth and a focus on those businesses where we can drive our own growth and create opportunities.

Pharmacia & Upjohn, Inc.

www.pnu.com

Mission

Pharmacia & Upjohn is a global, innovation-driven pharmaceutical company of 30,000 employees operating in more than 100 countries. Our products and our people demonstrate the company's commitment to improving wellness and quality of life around the world.

Profile

The company has a portfolio of leading prescription products, including Xalatan for glaucoma, Genotropin for the treatment of growth hormone deficiency and Detrol, an innovative therapy for overactive bladder. Pharmacia & Upjohn also markets over-the-counter products, including such household names as Rogaine, the hair loss treatment, and the Nicorette line of tobacco dependency products.

The scope of Pharmacia & Upjohn's pharmaceutical business includes prescription medications, consumer healthcare, animal health and sales of bulk pharmaceuticals. The company is also committed to research and development, investing about $1 billion a year annually. Areas of emphasis include oncology, metabolic disorders, infectious diseases and central nervous system disorders. Pharmacia & Upjohn also collaborates with other leading-edge companies to gain and apply technology in such areas as genomics and combinatorial chemistry.

Pharmacia & Upjohn has major research, manufacturing, and marketing operations in the United States, Sweden and Italy and subsidiaries in more than 50 other countries.

APPENDIX C

Rockwell International Corporation

www.rockwell.com

Mission

Rockwell is a world leader in electronic controls and communications. Our broad resources, commitment to quality and responsiveness are focused on our customers' success. Rockwell has two primary businesses—Rockwell Automation and Avionics & Communications, which includes Rockwell Collins and Rockwell Electronic Commerce. *The Rockwell Credo: What we believe* includes the following:

"We believe maximizing the satisfaction of our customers is our most important concern as a means of warranting their continued loyalty.... We believe the ultimate measure of our success is the ability to provide a superior value to our shareowners, balancing near term and long term objectives to achieve both competitive return on investment, and consistent increased market value."

Profile

The company employs nearly 40,000 persons. Its origins trace to when in 1903 Lynde Bradley and Dr. Stanton Allen formed Compression Rheostat Company (renamed Allen-Bradley in 1909) and when in 1919 Willard Rockwell bought a small axle plant called Wisconsin Parts Company to produce a new and improved axle based on his own designs. This company became Rockwell Spring and Axle in 1953, and following a merger with North American Aviation in 1967 became North American Rockwell. Subsequent acquisitions of Collins Radio, Allen-Bradley and Reliance Electric created the basis for Rockwell's world leadership in factory automation. During 1996–97 Rockwell sold or spun off various parts of its traditional business lines relating to aerospace-defense and automotive and acquired electronics and avionics enterprises to achieve its strategic restructuring into electronic controls and communication.

Sears, Roebuck and Co.

www.sears.com

Mission

Our strategy is to grow the company and create value by leveraging Sears unique strengths—our reputation for trust, integrity and fair value, as well as our excellent store locations, broad array of private and national brands, and proprietary credit card.

Profile

The company serves more than 60 million customer households nationwide, providing a wide range of apparel, home and automotive products and related services. Sears connects with American consumers through full-line and specialty stores, home services, direct response marketing and credit services. This unique combination of elements enables Sears to win in the marketplace by maintaining a relationship with customers through all the stages of their lives. Sears' key customer is the middle-income woman—and her family.

Wal-Mart Stores, Inc.

www.wal-mart.com

Mission

At its core, Wal-Mart is a place where prices are low and value and customer service are high—every day. Because Wal-Mart carefully controls expenses to maintain its low price structure, customers do not have to wait for a sale to realize savings.

Backing the hometown flavor of a Wal-Mart store is the industry's most efficient and sophisticated distribution system. The system allows each store to customize the merchandise assortment to match the community's needs.

Profile

Sam Walton (1918–1992) opened the first Wal-Mart store in 1962. The company Sam built has become the world's number one retailer. Diversification into grocery (Wal-Mart Supercenters), international operations, membership warehouse clubs (SAM'S Clubs), and deep discount warehouse outlets (Bud's Discount City) has created greater opportunities for growth. In 1995, the company created 85,000 new Wal-Mart jobs and supported thousands of U.S. manufacturing jobs. More than 600,000 Americans work at Wal-Mart.

Still, a key to Wal-Mart's popularity with consumers is its hometown identity. Shoppers are personally welcomed at the entrance by People Greeters. Locally-made merchandise is frequently and proudly displayed. Associates determine where charitable funds are donated. Sam Walton believed that each Wal-Mart store should reflect the values of its customers and support the vision they hold for their community.

Westvaco Corporation

www.westvaco.com

Mission

At Westvaco we provide customers with more value than they can obtain elsewhere by pursuing our proven strategy of product and service differentiation. Our strategy with its focus on value supports our objective to be the preferred supplier in each market we serve.

Our approach explains how we are strengthening Westvaco and serving key markets worldwide with differentiated products:

- Partnerships describes the value of our exceptional customer relationships and industry-leading research and development.
- Performance highlights how our services create value for customers and how an emphasis on value benefits our operations through better cost management.
- Products details our efforts to add value to Westvaco through product mix improvement.

- Preference looks at value in the form of preferred supplier relationships and market leadership.

Profile

Westvaco Corporation, a Delaware Corporation incorporated in 1899 as West Virginia Pulp and Paper Company, is one of the major producers of paper and paperboard in the United States. The company converts paper and paperboard into a variety of end-products, manufactures a variety of specialty chemicals, produces lumber, sells timber from its timberlands and is engaged in land development. In Brazil, it is a major producer of paperboard and corrugated packaging for the markets of that country and also operates a folding carton plant. Westvaco also has a folding carton plant in the Czech Republic and a joint venture in China. Westvaco exports products from the United States, Brazil and the Czech Republic to other countries throughout the world. International business accounts for 25 percent of sales and involves customers in more than 70 nations. Westvaco owns 1.5 million acres of timberland in the United States and Brazil.

APPENDIX D

Bibliography

AICPA Special Committee on Financial Reporting. 1993. *The Information Needs of Investors and Creditors*. New York: AICPA.

Amir, E. and B. Lev. 1996. Value-Relevance of Nonfinancial Information: The Wireless Communications Industry. *Journal of Accounting and Economics* 22: 3–30.

Barron, O. E., C. Kile, and T. O'Keefe. 1998. High-Quality MD&A. *Investor Relations Quarterly* Summer:17–21.

Boersema, J., and S. Van Weelden. 1992. *Financial Reporting for Segments.* Toronto: Canadian Institute of Chartered Accountants.

Bricker, R., Previts, G., Robinson, T., and Young, S. 1995. Financial Analyst Assessment of Company Earnings Quality. *Journal of Accounting, Auditing, and Finance* Summer.

Bryan, S. H. 1997. Incremental Information Content of Required Disclosures Contained in Management Discussion and Analysis. *Accounting Review* April:285–301.

Eccles, R. G., and H. D. Kahn. 1998. *Pursuing Value: The Information Reporting Gap in the U.S. Capital Markets.* New York: PricewaterhouseCoopers.

Eccles, R. G., and S. C. Mavrinac. 1995. Improving the Corporate Disclosure Process. *Sloan Management Review* Summer:11–25.

Epstein, M. J., and K. Palepu. 1999. What Financial Analysts Want. *IR Update*—National Investor Relations Institute Monthly Newsletter. May, 6–10.

FEI. 1993. Briefing—FEI Challenges Preliminary Findings of AICPA Special Committee. *FEI Briefing* October:1–2.

Financial Accounting Standards Board. 1998. *Business Reporting Research Project*. FASB.

APPENDIX D

Hill and Knowlton. 1984. *The Annual Report: A Question of Credibility*. New York: Hill and Knowlton.

Johnson, M. F., R. Kasznik, and K. Nelson. 1998. Speaking Out: A Look at the Effects of Safe Harbor on Disclosure Practices. *Investor Relations Quarterly* Summer:10–16.

Kerstein, J., and S. Kim. 1995. The Incremental Information-Content of Capital Expenditures. *Accounting Review* July:513–526.

Knutson, P. 1992. *Financial Reporting in the 1990's and Beyond: A Position Paper of the Association for Investment Management and Research.* Charlottesville, Va.: Association for Investment Management and Research.

Lee, T., and D. Tweedie. 1990. *Shareholder Use and Understanding of Financial Information.* New York: Garland Publishing.

Lee, T., and D. Tweedie. 1981. *The Institutional Investor and Financial Information*. London: The Institute of Chartered Accountants in England and Wales.

Lee, T., and D. Tweedie. 1977. *The Private Shareholder and the Corporate Report*. London: The Institute of Chartered Accountants in England and Wales.

Levitt, A. 1998. Remarks by Chairman Arthur Levitt, Securities and Exchange Commission, "The Numbers Game," NYU Center for Law and Business, New York, N.Y., September 28, 1998. New York, N.Y.: Securities and Exchange Commission.

Mahoney, B. May 1999. A Status Report on Use of the Safe Harbor. *IR Update*—National Investor Relations Institute Monthly Newsletter.

Mahoney, B. April 1999. Failure of Financial Reporting: Market Undervaluing Companies with Strong Knowledge Asset Base. *IR Update*—National Investor Relations Institute Monthly Newsletter.

Mahoney, B. February 1999. SEC Complaining Loudly on Current Accounting Practice. *IR Update*—National Investor Relations Institute Monthly Newsletter.

Bibliography

Mahoney, B. January 1999. Institutions Still Complaining About Quality of Information. *IR Update*—National Investor Relations Institute Monthly Newsletter.

Peterson, P. 1998. Measuring the Performance of Performance Measures. *Investor Relations Quarterly* Spring:15–23.

Previts, G., R. Bricker, T. Robinson, and S. Young, 1994. A Content Analysis of Sell-Side Financial Analyst Company Reports, *Accounting Horizons* June:55–70.

Previts, G., R. Bricker, T. Robinson, and S. Young. 1993. Financial Analysts' Use of Business Information. *Full Report of the AICPA Special Committee*. New York: AICPA.

Rimerman, T.W. 1990. The Changing Significance of Financial Statements. *Journal of Accountancy* April:79–83.

Rivel Research Group 1996. *An Analysis of Trends in the Practice of Investor Relations*. Vienna, Va.: National Investor Relations Institute.

Rogers, R., and J. Grant. 1997. Content Analysis of Information Cited in Reports of Sell-side Financial Analysts. *Journal of Financial Statement Analysis* Fall:17–31.

SRI International. 1987. *Investor Information Needs and the Annual Report*. Morristown, N.J.: Financial Executives Research Foundation, Inc.

Yurow, L. April 1999. What the SEC Has in Store for Your Periodic Reports. *IR Update*—National Investor Relations Institute Monthly Newsletter.

ABOUT THE AUTHORS

Julia Grant is an associate professor in the Department of Accountancy at the Weatherhead School of Management, Case Western Reserve University, where she also serves as director of the M.B.A. program. She earned her B.A. from the University of Arizona and her M.S. and Ph.D. from Cornell University. Her research and teaching interests include developing a greater understanding of how to effectively use financial information about a firm. These interests have led to several research projects examining the reports of financial analysts and the disclosure policies of corporations. She also has published several papers applying game theoretic social dilemma settings and studying their effects on group and policy outcomes. She has presented numerous refereed and invited papers, and has served on several American Accounting Association and Academy of Accounting Historians committees. She is a CPA and has served on the editorial advisory board of the *Ohio CPA Journal.*

Professor Grant is coeditor of the *Journal of Corporate Communications.* She is on the editorial board of *Research in Accounting Regulation* and serves as a referee for several other journals. She has also edited a book, *The New York State Society of Certified Public Accountants: Foundation for a Profession.* Her primary teaching responsibilities include the core accounting course in the MBA program and a doctoral seminar. She also participates in offering many executive development programs through the Dively Executive Education Center of the Weatherhead School of Management.

Timothy J. Fogarty is a professor in the Department of Accountancy at the Weatherhead School of Management, Case Western Reserve University. He is also the KPMG Peat Marwick Faculty Fellow at that school. He received a B.A., M.B.A., and J.D. from the State University of New York at Buffalo, an M.A. in economics and an M.A. in sociology from the University of North Carolina at Greensboro, and a Ph.D. from Penn State University. Before coming to Case Western Reserve, he taught at Penn State University and in the University of North Carolina system. He has published over 75 articles on a wide variety of topics in academic and practitioner journals. In addition to corporate communications and disclosures, his research interests include accounting education, the sociology of business organizations, and the regulation of professionals. He is the author of an auditing casebook used at many universities and colleges. He serves on the editorial boards of 10 journals, including several outside the United States. He has served in several capacities at the national level for the American Accounting Association (AAA), including president of the Public Interest Section and president of the Accounting, Behavior, and Organizations sections. At the Weatherhead School, he currently serves as department chair. He has been an attorney for over 20 years and a CPA for over 15 years. In addition to teaching business law, he has taught courses in income taxation, auditing, and accounting for undergraduate, graduate, and business executive students.

Robert Bricker, Ph.D., CPA, is an associate professor and Ernst and Young Faculty Fellow at the Weatherhead School of Management, Case Western Reserve University. He graduated with a B.A. from Baldwin Wallace in 1977 and a Ph.D. from Case Western in 1987. Professor Bricker has published over 40 articles in such leading journals as the *Journal of Finance, Financial Management, Journal of Accounting Research, Contemporary Accounting Research, Journal of Accounting, Auditing and Financing,* and *Accounting, Organizations and Society.* Professor Bricker is coeditor of the "Development of Accounting Thought" book series and of the *Journal of Corporate Communications.* He has presented refereed and invited papers at a variety of conferences, including the 1999 American Accounting Association annual meeting. He serves as the program director of the accounting doctoral program at the Weatherhead School. He is a member of and active contributor to several accounting-related professional and academic organizations, including the AICPA, AAA, and National Investor Relations Institute. His teaching interests are in financial accounting and corporate communications.

Gary Previts was appointed professor of accountancy at Case Western Reserve University in July 1979. He has served as chair of th- Department of Accountancy in the Weatherhead School and is cu- associate dean for undergraduate programs. Previousl- professor at the Culverhouse School of Accountancy. T- Alabama. He earned his undergraduate degree

University, his master's degree at The Ohio State University, and his Ph.D. at the University of Florida in 1972. A CPA, Previts has served as president of the Ohio Society of CPAs and on the board of directors of the AICPA. In 1996 he received the AICPA's Lifetime Achievement Award for Educators. He is the author of several books on the subject of accounting.

In 1991, Previts edited the proceedings monograph of the AICPA/Wharton School conference that initiated the Jenkins committee Project. He was the senior member of a project team of Case Western Reserve University researchers who investigated the content of sell-side analysts' reports under the sponsorship of the AICPA's Special Committee on Financial Reporting. In support of the Federal Accounting Standards Board's Business Reporting Research Project, he chairs the working party that has studied the reports of the automotive industry and the textile industry. He has served as a corporate consultant and an advisor to major accounting firms on matters relating to independence during the 1980s and 1990s. Presently he is a trustee of the AICPA Foundation. He also chairs a task force for the AICPA that is evaluating the standard-setting processes of the Federal Accounting Standards Advisory Board.

ACKNOWLEDGMENTS

We thank the people who have helped to make this work possible. We appreciate the assistance of Bill Sinnett, Rhona Ferling, and Jim Lewis of FERF, all of whom contributed in many ways to this outcome. We want to acknowledge the corporate members of our very knowledgeable and helpful advisory committee: Walter Wilson of EOG Resources, Inc., Robert Dickson of Carpenter Technology Corporation, and Earnie Edwards of Aluminum Company of America. They provided us with valuable information and feedback throughout the project. We also thank Janet Luallen of FEI, another member of the advisory group who was always available for assistance. Thanks go to the individuals at our sample firms who took the time to read a draft and provide feedback on this project. Finally, we thank Cheryl Strom, Sergey Dluzhevsky, and Santora Chin, very capable research assistants whose involvement improved this project.